not by chance
inspirational stories from gilbert, arizona

Two Rivers Church

Copyright © 2007 Good Catch Publishing, Beaverton, OR.

All rights reserved. Written permission must be secured from the publisher to use or reproduce any part of this book, except for brief quotations in critical reviews or articles.

This book was written for the express purpose of conveying the love and mercy of Jesus Christ. The statements in this book are substantially true; however, names and minor details have been changed to protect people and situations from accusation or incrimination.

All Scripture quotations, unless otherwise noted, are taken from the New International Version Copyright 1973, 1987, 1984 by International Bible Society

Published in Beaverton, Oregon, by Good Catch Publishing.
www.goodcatchpublishing.com
V1.1

Printed in the United States of America

Table of Contents

	dedication	9
	introduction	13
1	mr. right	15
2	becoming a man	47
3	fear failed	73
4	facing my demons	95
5	there with me	113
6	finally seeing clearly	141
7	home	165
	conclusion	191

dedication

This book is dedicated to the families who formed the core team that planted Two Rivers Church. Their faith in the Lord, their vision and their love for people has been key in how God has transformed so many lives.

Chad and Connie Awtrey
Kelly and Lindi Frieze
Shailesh and Aimee Ghimire
Kerry and Rhonda La Batt
Miguel and Pat Martinez
Ricardo Rivera
Nathan and Megan Rohde

We also salute those who have joined us along the way in this adventure. You make everything worthwhile. Together we look forward to the wonderful things the Lord has in store for us.

Thanks,
Tom and Theresa Alexander

The book you are about to read is a compilation of authentic life stories.
All the facts are true, all the events are real.
These storytellers have dealt with crisis, tragedy, abuse and neglect and have shared their most private moments, mess-ups and hang-ups in order for others to learn and grow from them.
In order to protect the identities of those involved in their pasts, the names of some storytellers have been withheld or changed.

introduction

Hope ... based on reality. We desperately need hope that comes from knowing of someone who has "faced a lion" and not only survived, but has found new life and the ability to share that new life with others.

The stories in this book that offer hope have not been modified or dramatized, nor exaggerated or inflated. They are stories of real people who either made less than ideal choices or were victims of insensitive and sometimes savage forces that brought them some of life's greatest difficulties. Their reports are wrenching, yet 100 percent true. In some cases, names of people or institutions have been changed to protect related parties from embarrassment by being unnecessarily exposed.

The fascinating part is how these broken people were able to make decisions that resulted in authentic life change. The individuals to whom these things happened are not idols, nor perfect people. They don't ride off into the sunset, never to encounter difficulty again. Rather, like everyone else, their past is like a haunting shadow and can still exert its influence in unguarded moments. Yet, in the midst of that, they have learned to overcome and press on by refocusing their attention on who transformed them — God.

We at Two Rivers Church offer these real-life stories, hoping to inspire and encourage you in your life's journey. God wants to accompany you. He is there. He is purposeful. Often, lives are radically transformed by seemingly

not by chance

random and meaningless events which turn out to be ... not by chance.

mr. right
the story of carla
written by christee wise

An organ brightly played the familiar notes of "The Bridal March." I could hear the swish of my gown and felt my father's warm right hand over mine resting in the crook of his left arm. My step dad stood to my right, pride welling in his eyes. My heart seemed to speed its rhythm as I carefully placed one satin-slippered foot in front of the other on the pristine aisle runner. *I wish that I was as pure as this white satin*, I thought.

I smiled at familiar faces, but my heartbeat was nearly frantic by the time I had passed three rows of smiling friends and teary-eyed family members. My mother's pleased face from near the front of the church encouraged me and saddened me at the same time.

If they knew, my thoughts accused, *if they only knew that I was marrying the wrong guy...*

I talked myself back under control.

No, Carla, don't think that way. Marrying Gary will make it right. It's too late to back out anyway. You'll look ridiculous if you leave now. Be tall. Stand proud.

"Too late. Too late." I woke myself with my own moaning.

"Ooohhh," I rolled over and groaned irritably into my pillow so that I wouldn't wake my roommate, Stacy, or Gary who was sacked out on the couch in our house. Dragging myself from bed, I made coffee and tried to push

not by chance

the recurring dream from my thoughts. I had a billion things to do today, not the least of which was a midterm test in anatomy at the University of Wyoming where I was studying for a degree in nursing. If I could get through that and a couple other classes, I had to go to work. Then, I needed to make some calls to confirm a couple details for the wedding just six weeks away and address some more invitations.

"Lord, help me," I continued to groan in the shower. It was a figure of speech that I hoped would bring some positive energy. Conversing with God wasn't a regular practice; I certainly had no reason to believe I'd earned his favor.

Moving from Lander between ninth and tenth grades was hard for me. I was a strong student, had many friends, and was involved in leadership activities and sports in Lander. In particular, I went to the state championships in gymnastics as a freshman. Our new town didn't even have a gymnastics program. But I played volleyball and the trauma of moving didn't affect my academic performance. School is one of the few things there is to do in a town of 1,500. Drinking and partying is another. Those of us who were approaching graduation began celebrating the summer before.

There were a couple of new faces in the crowd of about 30 at the bonfire one summer night at the lake. The sun went down, and the booze came out. The fire was crackling and sending sparks and flames up to provide lively, golden illumination to our party. We'd thrown some blan-

mr. right

kets around, roasted hotdogs and picnicked. The music was turned up and most everyone was dancing and laughing and having a great time.

"Oops! Sorry!" I replied as I bumped clumsily into what felt like a warm brick wall. The wall caught my smaller frame with strong arms.

"Whoa," the wall spoke quietly and helped me catch my balance on the mounded sand dance floor. Slowly, I looked from the wall's chest to his face. He smiled only slightly, but his brown eyes danced from under disobedient waves of dark hair escaping a worn cowboy hat.

"Gary," he said, tipping his hat with teasing cowboy etiquette.

"I'm Carla," I managed to speak. This cowboy was obviously not in high school. I tried not to let it show how taken I was with him. That he seemed to want to spend this evening getting to know me kindled my interest all the more.

Gary was four years older than me and incredibly good-looking. He was a professional bull rider or wanted to be. Though he was from the beginning very serious about me, I was still looking for fun and freedom during my last year in high school.

***

"What do you mean you're going to Homecoming with someone else? Why didn't you tell me? I'd take you." Gary wasn't taking this news well.

not by chance

"He's just a friend, Gary. I thought you'd be bored with the whole high school thing. I just want to have fun this year."

"What, you don't have fun with me?" He held my arm a little too tightly.

"I didn't mean that." I didn't want to hurt his feelings. I really liked him.

"Well, then, tell your little buddy that you're taken."

Every once in a while, Gary's possessiveness really bothered me. We'd only dated for a few months, and he thought he owned me. Something about this handsome, older man's attention distracted me and made me feel happy and special.

Socially vibrant and naturally outgoing, being alone was, for me as a teen, a torture close to death. Being with friends from school and other nearby towns drew me to parties and drinking on weekends.

My mother and stepfather were strong Christians and brought us up going to Sunday school and church. From my earliest memory, I had a desire to do the right thing and live a Christian life. At 3 ½ years old, I came to understand God's love for me and that Jesus died for my sins, for any wrong things I might do.

The social scene was still much more attractive than the options of church activities and groups for teens. In my heart, I truly desired to maintain the Christian values in which I'd been raised. I would never do drugs and was carefully saving myself physically for marriage. With these standards, I deceived myself that I was *not that bad* and

mr. right

was excused to make merry with as many friends as could be had on weekends.

My rationale was dangerously pitched.

Because I was only 18 months old when my parents split, I didn't suffer the more obvious bruises of the divorce. Far from negligent, my father exceeded his obligation in financial support. My sister and I had regular contact with our biological father though my brother was much older and went away to college before I was a teen. We got along well with our stepsisters, vacationing and enjoying fine outings and generous gifts. However, it seemed like my dad and stepmother fought often. In the long run, I came to realize I was content with a few less things and a little more relationship and peace.

I was unaware that the lack of special attachment to my father left a painful, empty place in my life. God could have filled it, had I let him.

It was January of my senior year in high school, and Gary and I were dating exclusively. Believing that we would be married, I gave myself to him physically.

I believed that because I *could* see myself marrying Gary, that I *would* marry him. This is one of Satan's traps. The biggest error in my thinking was that having sex with the guy you plan to marry is just about the same as waiting for marriage. Sadly, having slept with him cast more doubt on the relationship, not less. Rather than settling my heart, participating in sex before marriage compounded the issues. I suddenly felt bound to him because of our sexual relationship and more unable to part from him.

not by chance

I graduated that spring, second in my class of 30 students. This landed me a full-tuition scholarship to the University of Wyoming. I already knew that I wanted to go into nursing.

Disappointed and ashamed of myself for relinquishing my values, I hoped for a new beginning after graduation. We broke up and I spent the summer traveling, thinking in the fall that I'd head for U of W at Laramie and start over. But somehow we wound up back together.

Since Gary lived in Cheyenne, it wasn't difficult for me to go out occasionally behind his back. I did so frequently through my senior and then freshman year. I felt guilty but equally trapped and angry over his jealous rages.

"Why don't you just let him go?" Stacy suggested early the next year. She was the only one who ever knew how volatile the relationship was. We were housemates that second year at U of W.

"But I love him." I was convinced that's what I felt. "He doesn't mean to be that way. He can be very sweet and caring when he wants to."

"How can you know that he's going to *want* to be sweet when you're married?" Stacy had seen both sides of Gary. Now that we were engaged, he was at our house continually. She had walked in on us once when he had me pinned up against the wall. He pretended he was being playful, but she told me she'd heard him yelling before she came through the door. Endlessly, he badgered me about looking at or talking to other guys.

Gary and I married in May, in spite of my pre-wedding

mr. right

doubts and the recurring dream where I knew I was walking down the aisle to marry the wrong guy. Stacy's concern and my parents' suggestion of a longer engagement also weighed on my mind. They did not know the truth and generally liked the quiet young man when they'd met him.

***

It was a typical argument for us. Traveling down the road one day in his pickup, he said, "Give me some money. I need to gas up the truck."

"What happened to the money I gave you the other day?"

"Listen, I don't have to tell you anything about what I do with anything. It's *my* money. I work, too, ya know," he answered defensively.

"I know, but that's all we had for everything for the whole week."

"That's your problem; you're the one that said you have to handle the money."

"Because you can't … You bought pot with it, didn't you?" I reached for the glove compartment.

The truck veered to the left as he knocked my arm away. "You're really something, *Saint Carla*," he sneered, his voice filled with sarcasm. "You think you're so perfect."

As his anger escalated, his driving became more erratic and frightening.

not by chance

"Pull over!" I screamed. "I'll walk home."

To my shock and relief, he slammed on the brakes and slid into the gravel shoulder, barely stopping in time to stay out of the ditch. I slammed the door as I jumped out, feeling safer walking alone than riding with him.

Crash! I whirled back at the sound of breaking glass. Racing back to the truck, I saw the back window of the cab shattered. Arriving at home, he was incredulous about the broken window. In his rage, he'd gripped the steering wheel and thrown his head back against the window violently enough to smash the heavy glass. He had no idea.

Like that window, our relationship had the appearance of strength but repeatedly fractured on the impact of temper tantrums, jealousy, financial conflict, drug use and alcoholism.

One by one, my dreams were shattered. Some were fragile and fantastical to begin with. And I did my share of damage with the drinking and partying every weekend through high school and college. Desperate to repair cracks and fissures in my early daughter-father relationship, codependency regulated my inclination to reassemble the broken pieces in my marriage. I tried to keep the fragments together with social activity and stability in my career. My husband was a hard worker, but the large chip on his shoulder shadowed him from job to job. This, in fact, crushed yet another dream — that I would be able to stay home with children once they came.

After graduation, we moved to Colorado, where I pursued my student nursing at Fort Collins Hospital.

mr. right

***

Wild Willy's was already living up to its namesake when the wedding party had arrived. Gary was best man, and he'd already had plenty to drink at the reception. But partying and drinking, dancing and being with friends was what weekends were for, and we were ready to go all night long. I'd just bumped into some old friends that weren't from the wedding and was catching up with them.

"Easy, guys!" I heard someone utter loudly enough to be heard over the din.

I turned and peered through the seething mass of cowboy hats and denim. My heart leapt into my throat.

Western music poured from the speakers in the ceiling, and the revelers bounced and jostled to the beat. A big commotion was kicking up in one corner of the rustic barroom. Instinctively, I knew Gary was in the thick of it.

Like a pint-sized linebacker, I pushed my way through the crowd to my husband's side, where he was already facing off with a man from India. Gary was taller and the other guy was weighing the worth of engaging.

"Please let it go," I begged. "Gary, please." I could see that he couldn't hear me, though I was standing right next to him. I grasped his arm, hoping that somehow a touch or word from me might break through the rage-induced trance he was in. He shrugged me off like I was nothing.

Both of them had their chests puffed out and fists doubled. The crowd was widening to form a boxing ring. The bartender growled loudly, "Take it outside. I'm calling the

not by chance

cops."

Julie and Jeff, the friends with whom I had ridden to the bar, popped out of the crowd behind me and stood on either side of me.

"Gary, c'mon," I urged. "It's not worth it. You've had too much to drink."

I thought for a split second he was listening — he started to take a step back and so did the Indian. Suddenly, Gary lifted the corner of a nearby table and slammed it back down, blurting a racial slur and looking for it to take effect. His antagonism hit its mark and the opponent lunged. Satisfaction flashed in Gary's eyes as some bystanders grabbed hold of his furious adversary. The crowd used its strength to push the two challengers toward the door, spilling the fight into the street. I dashed for another exit in hopes of preventing further disgrace. Julie and Jeff followed. They had already witnessed Gary's indifference to me. The situation was rapidly getting out of hand.

I couldn't catch him, and so I yelled at him from a short distance, "Gary, do you hear me? I'm leaving!" I turned on my heel to head down the street. Flashing red and blue lights raced around the corner and skidded to a stop. I was mortified.

"Don't you walk away from me," Gary's voice seemed to echo off the street.

I kept walking.

Suddenly, my head jerked back as a strong hand grabbed my hair and neck in one big handful. I gasped as I stumbled backward in pain. I didn't think Gary had even

mr. right

heard me, he was so enraged. Now, he slammed me against the brick wall between storefronts and repeated the threat.

"Don't you EVER walk away," he snarled in my face, as he held me against the building, my feet hardly staying in touch with the pavement.

I gathered all of my strength to resist and break free. Two officers were already pulling Gary away from me. I lurched forward at the release, and one of them steadied me.

"You okay?" he asked.

Tears threatened. I was shaken, but I was already trying to salvage my pride, "Yes, I'm fine. Thank you."

"Would you like to tell me what happened?" the officer questioned.

"It was nothing really. We just need to go home," I hedged.

"We? You know him?"

"He's my husband."

"Well, we can get you a ride home, ma'am, but he's been arrested."

"No. NO!" I began to argue. I saw another policeman speaking with Jeff and Julie.

What must they be thinking of all this?

"It's just a misunderstanding. I'm not pressing charges."

"Ma'am, it really doesn't matter whether you want to press charges or not. Your husband has been arrested based on what we saw happen. Maybe you'd like to let him

not by chance

sleep it off tonight at the jail." The officer made it sound like they were doing me a favor.

"No!"

As soon as they hauled Gary away, I sprung into action to fix the problem. My mission was twofold, damage control and self-preservation. First, I had to make sure Jeff and Julie and all the rest knew this was a terrible misunderstanding and an isolated incident. Second, I could leave no room for Gary to accuse and punish me for disloyalty. My humiliation at this moment was nothing compared to the hell I would pay if he was disrespected. Though he'd brought this upon us, I knew I was the guardian of our reputations.

I hurried to the ATM machine by the bar, while Julie and Jeff tailed me in concern. The cash supply in the machine had been depleted by the thirsty crowd in anticipation of last call at the bar.

"Gotta find Ryan." I faced Julie with a plea for help. Ryan was Gary's cousin, and I felt certain he could help. We could keep this contained.

Ryan loaned me the money to post bail, and we raced to the jail. To my surprise, Gary wasn't there. He'd been released before we arrived. Jeff and Julie suggested they drive me home, and I was too tired to argue, even though I knew things could get worse. First, we returned to the bar to give back the money I had borrowed.

Pulling into the drive, I spotted Mr. Reardon's familiar blue truck. Mr. Reardon was the father of one of Gary's good friends. Gary had lost his own father to liver disease

mr. right

when he was just a senior in high school. Mr. Reardon filled some of the void. A wordless sigh of dismay escaped me and betrayed my sorrow and defeat. Shame sealed everything, causing me to send all three of our friends away, despite their strong arguments to stay for my sake.

The back door had been broken and shards of glass lay on the patio. Apparently, Gary had already attempted to enter. My anger reached a new level. Gary was too drunk and I was too hurt, humiliated, ashamed and angry to speak, and we went to bed in silence.

The next day, the anger was replaced with overwhelming sorrow, as I swept up the pieces of broken glass, knowing that there was no way to put things back together. Attempts were made at counseling over the next few weeks and months. I concentrated on avoiding conflict and hoped for change. I soon recognized that it wasn't going to happen. We had been together, including dating and marriage, for six years, and I struggled to see any hope in sight. I was holding on to slivers and sand. The more I tried, the more it slipped away or punctured and ground at tender parts of me.

"Gary, it's over. I've had enough," I finally announced.

He stared at me dumbly. I had packed my bag and loaded my car, thinking that I may have to leave in secret.

He wasn't taking me seriously.

"It's over, Gary," I repeated. "I don't want to put up with the temper, the lying, the spending money all the time, the belittling, the abuse," I replied. "I won't. I want a separation." The "D" word was still beyond me.

not by chance

I pulled into my mother and step dad's house as the digital clock on the dashboard flashed 11:52 p.m. I watched as the minutes blinked by one at a time until it was 12 a.m. That was my curfew on weekends when I was 15. Making curfew had helped me conceal the partying and drinking.

Then I turned and stared at the house. In all my years with Gary, I had never once gone home after one of our fights. Mom and I had always been close, but there were many secrets she never knew. Now, I was going to shock her with the heartbreaking news of my failing marriage. Closing my eyes, I imagined her standing in the earthy-toned kitchen when I was a teen, saying, "I love you, Carla. I'm so proud of you."

Tears plopped onto my hands in my lap. I wiped them on my pants and then placed my hands atop the steering wheel, leaned my head against it and wept. My heart ached with shame and grief.

I pulled back the lever and opened the door. It took all of my strength to walk up the sidewalk, and I sat on the stoop to consider my words. I couldn't imagine, as I gathered my courage to face my parents, how they might respond. My fear was that once the door opened the whole truth would come spilling out.

The sun was beginning to rise and turn the sky a funny color. It was time.

"Carla!" my mother wrapped me up in her arms. "What's happened? Are you all right?"

"I'm so sorry, Mom. I'm so sorry," I choked.

mr. right

"Sorry?" she pulled me into the house.

"I have to leave Gary. I can't take it anymore. He's never going to change, and I'm tired of lying and trying to hide it. Our marriage is a fake. What everyone sees is not real," I managed. "I can't stay with him. I made a huge mistake ... I'm so sorry."

"It's okay, it's okay," she said over and over, as she stroked my back the way she did to comfort me when I was a child. She immediately whispered, "Jesus, help us. It's okay. Jesus, help us."

She held me a long time that way. Finally, she led me to the kitchen table.

"Cocoa or tea?"

"Cocoa," I whispered, already feeling the relief of confession.

She sat across from me and held my hands in hers. Her eyes filled with tears.

"I knew you were unhappy, sweetheart. I just didn't know why. The truth will set you free, Carla."

It did.

My mother's strong faith comforted and filled me. How could I have been so close to her for so long and yet be so afraid to let her know the agony of my marriage? How could I have missed that she too had been through similar struggles?

I had to go back to work a few days later. Gary went to stay with my cousin, the pastor. That puzzled me, but I wanted him out of the house. I was afraid that he'd gain control of me again.

not by chance

Every few days, I'd arrive home and find that Gary had sabotaged or taken something. He unplugged the fridge and freezer. Everything spoiled. Then the unnerving incidents stopped ... for about a week.

"Hello, *wife*." I awoke about 5:30 a.m. to see Gary leering at me from the edge of my bed. His words dripped with anger and bitterness.

I was paralyzed with fear. He could kill me.

He unfastened his belt and jeans and crept onto the bed toward me. Our eyes locked. We both knew I was no match for his powerful build or blinding rage. I calculated my chances of reaching the bedroom door, let alone the neighbors, for help.

"We are going to have sex, Carla." My legs were pinned under the covers, and he was forcibly removing my pajama top. "If you're pregnant, you'll never leave me. Is that what you want?"

His tone and look were so evil that I remembered nothing of the man I once loved. I was repulsed and terrified. With no time to confess my sin, my unworthiness forgotten, I cried out, "Jesus, help me!"

I was sobbing and twisting my face from this stranger, struggling fiercely to get away. He was trying to force me to have sex, and in my mind, it was rape. Rape is about power and control, and that's all Gary wanted.

He'd placed his right forearm across my chest to hold me down while he tore at the covers and my pajamas. Suddenly, he froze.

Staring into my eyes, he said, "What did you say?"

mr. right

The weight across me lifted ever so slightly, and I gathered a fragment of courage from an unknown source.

"Jesus, help me," I repeated with more authority.

Like rewinding a movie, he was off the bed, dressed and leaving me as quickly as he'd appeared.

I stumbled to the front door. It was locked. Confused, I rushed to the back door and found it ajar. He must have left it unlocked for himself during one of his previous raids. I shut and locked it, then leaned back against it, closed my eyes and took a deep breath. The phone gave me a start.

"H-hello." I tried to sound normal.

It was the associate pastor at the church. Gary had been doing some counseling with him and his wife.

"Are you okay?"

"Yes, I'm fine." I felt a twinge of irritation. Though I knew he'd been sincere in his attempt to help Gary, having provided refuge to my aggressor during our separation felt like betrayal. I did not wish to talk with him and secured my privacy with brevity on the phone, just as I had shut and locked the door seconds before.

Gary had apparently been overcome with guilt and rushed to the pastor to confess immediately.

It was a long time before I began to feel safe again. I immediately asked a girlfriend to move in with me. Gary eventually moved back to Wyoming. We were divorced, and it became final about six and a half years from the night of the bonfire.

Four or five months had passed since Gary moved out.

not by chance

I started going out with friends and enjoying a social life again when I met Lance. His willingness to do anything for me was refreshing. Lance adored me. I liked being treated well and living without fear.

Though my social life centered around bars and parties, I began to see that perhaps God desired more of my attention than spastic allegiance. I considered seeking his approval of this relationship. To me, that approval was granted in the form of goodness. Lance was good to me. He said that he was a Christian, and there was no reason to doubt him. After all, Gary said he'd accepted Jesus as savior. At least Lance's treatment of me was a measure of proof.

When Lance asked me to marry him, I said yes.

Lance's sister, Amy, had just turned 21. Always up for a party, several mutual friends and I took her to The Wagon Wheel to celebrate. Feeling happy and friendly, we invited everyone we saw that night to buy her a drink.

"Hi," I smiled to a nice looking guy that caught my eye as everyone seemed to be mingling in the bar. "This is Amy. It's her 21st birthday. Would you like to buy her a drink?"

He looked amused. "Okay, I guess so. Happy Birthday, Amy! What's your friend's name?"

"Oh, I'm Carla. Yours?"

"I'm Rick."

He bought the beer, and we all clanked our glasses together to make the most of the tradition.

I found out that Rick was a veterinarian working on

mr. right

his PhD in biomedical science in Fort Collins. I told him that I was in medicine, too, but I was a "people" nurse. We soon discovered several other things that we had in common. He was divorced. We had both been raised in the church and considered ourselves to be Christians. I told him that I was engaged, but we spent all night perched on bar stools, talking like old friends.

The house gradually emptied. Early the next morning, we parted company. I never really thought that I would see him again, but he mentioned that if I ever wanted to get in touch with him, I could reach him at the veterinary school.

Not long after this, Lance and I had an unusual disagreement and split up. Lance was crushed. He became depressed and couldn't stay in the same town, knowing I was there.

I called my mom to break the news.

She wasn't surprised. "Carla, I've been praying a lot about you and Lance. I'm not sure he's the one for you."

Mom had been praying for me all my life. She would never interfere or tell us what to do or what not to do. She'd just pray. I somehow knew it was very important, and for the most part, was glad that she spent time in prayer for me. It worked for her, and I decided I'd try it a little more myself.

My thoughts automatically turned to the cute, aspiring veterinarian that I met at the bar. Late one evening, I called the vet school wondering if there was any chance he'd be there. To my surprise, he answered and he remem-

not by chance

bered me. He had worked late and was ready to eat, so we met at a restaurant. We stayed till the restaurant closed at 11 p.m.

Having worked the graveyard shift at the hospital for several weeks, I was just then beginning to get hungry, so we found another restaurant where we continued talking through my dinner and the night.

From the beginning, we felt terrifically connected and compatible. A deep friendship formed quickly. A few months later, still not convicted about sexual purity and holiness, we became sexually involved.

One of the commonalities that Rick and I shared was that we had been raised in Christian homes. I told Rick of my desire to follow Christian values and to get to know God better.

"I respect you, Carla," he said, "but I am not ready to put my trust in a God who would allow the things I've been through in the last few years." He had struggled through a six-year marriage that had devolved to the level of mere coexistence as they both poured themselves into their careers. More recently, his mother's unexpected death from a car accident at age 53 left him with bitter grief.

Weeks went by, and it was time to move forward in or out of the relationship.

Rick was studying with a world-renowned horse surgeon who was investing himself into Rick as a long-awaited protégé. This predecessor was so remarkable that it was easy for a chosen student such as Rick to adopt not

mr. right

only his skills but some of his philosophy of life, as well. Dr. Burgett's wife was successful in her career as well, and they had no children. His career was thus the focal point of his life, and Rick was moving in the same direction.

Realizing that my desire for marriage and family exceeded his, we broke up.

I returned to Lance, thinking that the man who loved me so completely must be the right one. Lance received me with open arms.

***

"Hi, Carla. It's me, Rick."

My heart skipped a beat. "Hi! How are you?" my voice betrayed my enthusiasm at hearing his voice.

"Actually, I'm doing great. That's why I'm calling. Carla, some things have happened, and I wanted to tell someone ... I wanted to tell *you*."

This was a real surprise, and I wasn't quite sure how to handle it. Rick and I had shared an easy communication, but for the first time, I questioned how an engaged Christian woman should receive a male friend.

"Wow, you sound so excited. I'd love to see you. Um, Rick, I'm engaged ... to Lance," I finally managed.

"Oh," he paused, "congratulations."

I plunged forward. "But what is it you wanted to tell me?"

"I'd really like to see you. Can we meet?"

The next day, I paced my small living space as I waited.

not by chance

I checked the clock and then practiced what I might say and what I might do when I saw him. I tried to imagine what he might say. Fifteen minutes past the hour and no Rick. I looked out the front window and then flopped down in an easy chair with a magazine. I stared at the pages. I jumped back up and paced some more. Half past and no Rick.

Maybe he's changed his mind because I'm engaged. That's too bad, I thought.

When an hour had gone by, I sighed deeply and forced myself to take on a load of laundry to assuage my disappointment.

The phone rang. It was Rick.

"I'm sorry; my truck broke down and won't start. Could you pick me up at the Chevron on Washington?"

By the time I had picked him up and driven him back to his disabled vehicle, it roared to life without hesitation. *How strange. God, what are you doing?* I thought.

We sat in his truck, and he told me his story.

"I was in the lab late at night. No one else was around. I was working on some research that has been demanding my attention. I started to become aware of the emptiness of my surroundings — the clock ticking, the silence, the darkness except for the area I was in and I thought, 'What am I doing?' I began to realize I could spend my whole life becoming a great surgeon or researcher and still be all alone. I was completely overcome. There I was, weeping in the lab."

My eyes filled with tears as I heard the depth of convic-

mr. right

tion in his voice.

"I finally gave up what I was working on and went home. When I got home, I picked up the newspaper and opened it without thinking. There was a full-page spread about the Easter service at that church where we went that one time … do you remember? The one where I was mad because the preacher talked about money?"

I nodded. Of course, I remembered. It was a Vineyard church I attended regularly. I'd thought, *Oh, brother. The one day I talk Rick into going with me and Pastor talks about money. He never talks about money.*

He continued, "I went to the Easter service. I have no idea why. I don't remember what he talked about this time. But at the end, he started pointing people out in the crowd and saying that God was saying this or that. It was kind of freaking me out," he admitted.

Rick was raised Baptist, so I knew how weird, even frightening, it may have felt to him when some Pentecostals began, as they would call it, "operating in the gifts."

"He was saying, 'There's someone over here in this section that needs prayer. God loves you. He wants to do something for you, today.' Then he pointed right at me. I knew that God was trying to speak to me. So I went forward for prayer."

Blinking back tears and swallowing at the lump in my throat, I stared at my hands in my lap. I was thrilled for him and filled with a desire to have the same kind of relationship with God. I also wanted a husband who loved the Lord and heard his voice.

not by chance

"Carla, I rededicated my life to God. I've been attending a small home group, and I've been growing and asking the Lord what he wants for my life."

I was falling apart.

He went on, "I think that we're meant to be together. But if we're not, I want you to at least know that being with God is the most important thing of all."

I could not find my voice. We sat in silence for a full minute.

At the very same moment, we both began to speak. I started, "Ri …"

He started, "Car …" and stopped.

"Rick, I can't make any decisions. I've messed up so many times. I'm with Lance, and that's where I'm staying unless God says something different." I knew Lance would never change his mind, but now my heart was being torn in two.

There was only one way the pieces could be put back together. I went home and laid my life before the Lord.

"God? This is it. I absolutely will not make a move unless you show me what to do. You will have to direct me. You will have to guide me. I'm with Lance unless you make it clear that you have something else for me," I prayed earnestly. I felt strange inviting God into this part of my life, but I couldn't afford the grief of another mistake.

Lance and I had a date that Friday night.

I stared at the man, my fiancé, in disbelief. "Carla." Lance had met me at the door of his house in Denver. "It's

mr. right

over. I know you're not happy. This ... us ... we — it's not going to work."

"I don't understand."

"Don't call and don't come by. It's over."

I was speechless.

"Goodbye." He closed the door.

To prove to myself that it was real, I finally reached out and touched the door with my fingertips. "Goodbye," I whispered.

Stunned, I went to my car. I sat for several minutes just staring at the steering wheel, pondering my feelings. Sad, but not brokenhearted, relieved, but not rejoicing, I started the engine.

Not only had the plans for the evening changed, but my life plans had suddenly vaporized. I felt untied. Since I didn't know what else to do, I headed toward Highway 25 and home.

It was a beautiful drive from Denver to Fort Collins. My car knew it well, and the weather was pleasant that June evening as the sun began to fall behind the foothills. I let my mind wander over the strange encounter with Lance.

Without warning, a deer appeared from the shadows not 100 feet in front of my car. Fighting the urge to slam on the brakes, I avoided putting the Saturn into a skid. A rush of adrenalin flooded my system, and everything went into slow motion. I pumped the brakes and steered to the left. The startled animal turned the same way, and my margin to adjust slipped away. I swung right, just in time

not by chance

to miss her.

"Carla, just as I am in control of this situation right now, I am in control of what happened with Lance." It was a voice I hadn't heard for a very long time but recognized immediately.

Instantly, I knew that I would never be the same. The words were too strong, too specific, too quick for me to have dreamed them up myself. They had penetrated the thundering of my own heart, calmed it and then set it beating wildly again with wonder.

God had spoken to *me,* about *my* life. He had not given me up as a lost cause.

As I brought the vehicle back into the lane, I placed my life into the hands of the one who had spared it. I glanced in my rearview mirror and watched the beautiful doe amble into the trees. Before my pulse returned to normal, I thanked God for protecting me both in body and in spirit.

The Lord removed my shame over my mistakes and gave me hope enough to begin talking to him frequently.

A few days later, I heard him again. "I am giving Rick to you. It's okay for you to be together, but don't ever withhold him from me."

***

In the late afternoon, Lake Loveland perfectly reflected the wooded mountainside. The aspens were still green and, in early September, only hinted at donning their fall colors. Rick and I waded, hand in hand, until the clear wa-

mr. right

ter reached our knees.

"This is so beautiful," I exclaimed. "It's just how I imagined it but better."

"Mm-hmm," he affirmed, looking at me.

We faced each other and smiled. My cousin, the pastor, was talking with some of our friends at the water's edge as he prepared to wade in. He looked our way and grinning, asked, "How is it?"

"Perfect," we both replied.

People from the church were still arranging their picnic goods up in the table area. We leaned our heads together and reaffirmed our love for each other and the Lord. Rick prayed a prayer of thanksgiving. He said "amen" just as my cousin, also the pastor, swished his way over to join us. My cousin's presence was so significant because he knew all about my marriage and divorce and saw the miracle of God bringing Rick and me together.

Before he baptized Rick, my cousin explained, "When Rick goes down under the water, it symbolizes the death of Christ in our place and the death and burial of our old selves with him. The water represents Jesus' blood washing our sins away; being brought up out of the water shows that we are raised with Christ to live a new life, one that's pleasing to him."

I had never been baptized to show my commitment to the Lord. Rick wanted to be re-baptized since he recommitted his life to the Lord. He accepted Christ and was baptized in the Baptist church when he was 9. He had a relationship with the Lord through his teen years, and

not by chance

then, after a couple of tumultuous events in his early 20s, drifted away. His divorce and his mom's death added fuel to excuse his drifting. Now, together, he wanted us to commit our lives and share our cleansing.

Rick helped arrange for us to be baptized in the lake. He had heard me say how much I wanted it to be this way. After he was baptized, he and my cousin baptized me. This confirmed that he would lead the way in moving closer to the Lord. He'd begun by committing with me to reserve sex until we were married. God really convicted both of us on the subject of purity and holiness and our bodies being the Lord's. Even though we both had been married before and had enjoyed other sexual relationships, God showed us that we could be pure, white as snow, before him again.

We soon realized that sin truly is washed away by God's forgiveness.

On September 2, 1995, I walked down the center aisle of a church again. This time, I wore white on the outside *and* the inside. Jesus had made me pure.

With Gary, I had disregarded the Lord's instruction.

With Lance, I asked merely for God's approval and blessing upon *my* choice.

But when I let God choose a partner for me, his choice was perfect.

Rick and my cousin both smiled confidently from the front as I approached. Not a single doubt darkened the moment, nor has it since. The answer to my emptiness was not the right guy, it was the right God. It was relying

mr. right

on God, asking him for guidance and being obedient to follow. As both of us pursued God to fill us, we find ourselves daily growing closer to each other.

In the midst of my struggle to find my way back to the Lord, my mother shared a Bible verse with me out of Psalm 37. It reads, "Delight yourself in the Lord, and he shall give you the desires of your heart."

My desire was always to have a family. God has given Rick and me three beautiful reminders of restoration, healing and blessing for delighting in him. Rick is a wonderful father and spiritual leader. Skilled and dedicated in his profession as an equine surgeon, we are both thankful that I can be at home with the children full-time.

Picking up the pieces of broken dreams left us both with cuts and scrapes and a knowledge that those things can never be reclaimed. But it has also made us compassionate and understanding as we see young people searching and besieged with temptation. God has given us a new dream of leading others to him for healing.

We have other dreams, like seeing new churches born, raised and growing. Just like the number of children, we've helped build three new churches. Each new leadership opportunity and dream has been followed by God equipping us for the task.

God has, through Rick's wisdom and quiet strength, ministered healing to many of my wounds. Every time I see Rick interact with our daughter, my newly healed heart just sings, because I didn't have a close relationship like that with either of my dads. It brings healing to know that

not by chance

she will have that security of a great, godly father who loves her.

We've, in turn, opened our home and hearts to teach and lead others in small home groups. My love for socializing and Rick's kindness and gift of teaching make us a great team.

My suffering has identified me with Christ and made me more appreciative of God's grace and forgiveness. Rick and I have been privileged to pray and minister to numerous individuals and couples in their marriages.

***

I stood in the lobby of Two Rivers Church in Gilbert, Arizona, greeting newcomers and introducing them to people all around me. I heard the worship team warming up on the platform and Rick tuning his guitar. My heart swelled with love and happiness as I entered the auditorium, already filling with worshipers. Rick caught my eye, and I knew we were in the same open place before God, ready to be used.

Soon, everyone was standing and clapping and singing praises to the Lord. At prayer time, we went forward and prayed with a handful of men and women. Rick spent several minutes encouraging a young man dealing with depression. I saw him put his hand on the man's shoulder, listening carefully as the distressed man poured out his heart. I knew we'd be praying for him again at home during the week and Rick might take him out for coffee.

mr. right

I found the kids playing outside and headed for the car.

Now, it's Sunday afternoon. It's warm and there is dancing and partying by the pool. The children and their friends are dancing around in their swimsuits, that is. The grownups talk and laugh and raise glasses of iced tea.

"Can we get in yet?" our youngest pleads.

"Wait for Dad," I call and turn to Rick. "Thanks for helping with the dishes, but I think you'd better get out there."

He gives me a quick hug and a kiss on the cheek, then pauses to tease me in low tones, "Can't wait to see you in that new swimsuit."

Thank you, God, for making us right.

becoming a man
the story of aaron gochee
written by christee wise

When it began, I wasn't quite 12. My mother was 27, and Kim, her lesbian lover, was 21.

"We would like to have a child, Aaron," Mom began, "together."

She hurried on, "We want that child to be linked to both of us by blood."

"We need you to help," Kim chimed in, her blue eyes glassy. I knew she'd been drinking. She pushed her straight blonde hair behind her ears and tried to find something or someone to focus on. Her hands kept twisting at the pillow in her lap.

Just seconds ago, I'd clicked the pause button on the video game I was playing. When I'd heard Mom call my name and ask me to come into her room, I expected the usual, "Have you finished your homework? How 'bout your chores?"

I was ready for the typical exchange tonight. She was fairly strict. I was characteristically obedient in those two areas. We were in sync that way.

It took me a moment to make the mental leap from what I was expecting to hear to what I was actually hearing. Slowly, it dawned on me that they weren't just asking, "What would you say to having a little brother or sister?" That in itself was a question that had never even crossed my mind.

not by chance

My mother was 16 when she had me. My father had disappeared shortly after she discovered she was pregnant. I've been told he reappeared the day I was born demanding, "You're going to name that baby after me, aren't you?"

"No," she answered flatly.

As before my birth, he was never around afterward, either, despite my mother's repeated efforts to get him involved.

She raised me without much support from anywhere, since she'd had little herself. Accidentally escaping from an abusive home as a teenager caused her to try her best to do a good job with me. Nevertheless, we were children helping each other survive, taking turns being strong at different times. We were buddies.

Our relationship was altered when she and Kim hooked up. I was about 7 or 8 years old when Kim moved in with us. To my knowledge, the family was complete even if it was not conventional.

"How?" I directed the question at my mother. In my mind, I was assembling a puzzle and I needed more pieces. Kim seemed distracted and that irritated me. There was a knot forming in my stomach.

"Well, you could be the link for me," Mom spoke carefully and took my hand and pulled me over to sit beside her. At the same time, Kim reached over and took Mom's other hand. We sat in a strange triangle on the bed in their shared room.

I stared back at my mom, stilled confused by what they

becoming a man

were getting at. With the scene still unfolding, funny signals went off in my head. Something was "off" about their invitation.

I blinked and stole a glance at the young woman who was, by role, my stepparent. She was not really old enough to be my parent — maybe an older sister — and whether stepparent or sibling, her involvement with my mom struck me as an intrusion and a weak basis for any authority over me.

Yet Kim was a young woman, my mom's partner. The trio that sat on the bed that evening discussing how to make a baby was a toxic mix of youth, hormones and rebellion.

"Link?" I repeated.

"Yeah, donor," Kim offered.

Mom quickly began to explain, "Kim can have a baby for us if you donate your sperm ..."

I felt dizzy. Although I was mature for my age and well informed about sex, it took a full minute to realize what they were proposing. Were they serious? They were obviously feeling the happy and relaxing effects of sharing a bottle of wine. They were giddy with excitement about their plan.

Meanwhile, having broken the ice with me, they rattled on openly about the two options I had for participation. I stared at the blue-green zigzag pattern in the bedspread. The dizziness grew worse, and the zigzags began to move and play tricks on my eyes. Was I dreaming? I squeezed my eyes shut to try to clear my head, then looked

not by chance

up, concentrating hard on my mother's words. As the truth began to sink in, I sensed myself being pulled into a different relationship with the two of them. This conversation as a rite of passage stirred me in an unsettling way.

We talked for more than an hour but never discussed how this would change the already complicated relationships in our home, potentially adding new ones. Would this child make me a father or a brother? I never asked. At the moment, it was a matter of negotiating the physical details of their scheme. For me, that meant making a choice between having sex with a grown woman and agreeing to some nebulous procedure involving a clinic.

Curious as any other 12-year-old man-child, I was also intelligent and mature for my age. I saw no reason not to participate. The most natural and enticing option for me as a preteen was to sleep with Kim. Lacking any religious guidelines, I was full-on agnostic, if anything. I didn't believe in God or the devil. If they existed, I was of little consequence to them, and so was my behavior. My mother was a loving parent, stricter than many of my friends' parents. She'd always leveled with me on things. It never occurred to me that the proposal they were making might be illegal.

Fortunately, a child was not conceived that night or any of the times Kim conducted relations with me over the next couple of years.

But instantaneously and forever, roles in our house were scrambled. I had crossed a line into manhood to a degree without a male role model. At first, I had no com-

becoming a man

prehension of being used. Over time, it grew apparent that I was only the man of the house for expedience in one context, as though I'd been invited into the club and then summarily dismissed from it.

My mother was filled with remorse immediately. The next day, with the influence of prescription drugs and alcohol passing, she began to confess her regret to me. Many times she told me, "I'm so sorry for putting you through that. It was a terrible mistake."

Her contrition was complete in that for 10 years after the fact, she only knew of the one instance. She never knew that having been exposed, I was a vulnerable target for her lover. Beyond that, the normal sexual desire in me was fuelled, ignited and would burn with ever-increasing intensity to be satisfied.

Guilt and jealousy battled for my heart as the "secret relationship" continued until I was in the eighth grade. The guilt was an incredible burden to bear. My mother's repentance suggested that I, too, could reverse direction, but I didn't. This increased my shame. A sense of responsibility and the constant threat of alienation as a consequence of my treachery insured my silence. The jealousy arose when I'd see them together, laughing, talking, holding hands, though I could never speak or even sort out my feelings.

"No!" I yelled angrily, "I'm not going to pick up your stupid crap."

Kim stood with her hands on her hips, ordering me to clean up the house. Truth was Mom had given me the list

not by chance

of chores before she left for work. But I wasn't going to take any orders from this woman who was my ... my ... what was she to me?

"Come on, buddy." She tried a different tactic and put her hand on my arm, a touch that struck a match to a powder keg.

I cut her off.

"I'm not your buddy, and I'm not your kid! Get the hell away from me, you ..." I jerked loose with an expletive, giving her a nudge as I headed for the door. Two years had empowered me with height, wisdom and plenty of anger. I was done playing games with her, and I was almost as disgusted with her as I was with myself.

Down the block, it took no longer than five minutes to find some friends with an equal or larger amount of rebellion and umbrage. Our high school teachers called us "at-risk youth," peers called us "burnouts," parents labeled us "bad influences" and "troublemakers," but to each other, we were a brotherhood of the oppressed. We gathered on a vacant lot, behind some overgrown brush and passed cigarettes and war stories. We respectfully spared each other the details. We were like wounded soldiers in an understaffed field hospital. Ill equipped to administer any real first aid, our injuries were more severe than any of us could handle.

Mom spotted me on her way home from work and heard Kim's side of the story before I arrived. Alarmed by my attitude and choice of friends, Mom made arrangements for me to see the school counselor. They wanted to

becoming a man

determine the reason for my struggle with authority, particularly in regards to my mother's partner. However, when the cause was revealed, at least in part, the counselor had a legal obligation to report sexual abuse.

At 14 years old, to be a high school freshman escorted from school by the police in front of your friends is humiliating. Far more confusing and frightening is to be placed in a *shelter* with dozens of juvenile delinquents. Two days passed, then the one-week maximum for shelter residents prior to placement in foster care. I was in this loosely named *shelter* for more than a month. In that time, there was only one other person besides myself that was brought in as a victim of someone else's crime, rather than his own. The time I spent there felt much like serving a sentence. By the time foster care opened up for me, I emerged from the place fairly jaded and able to take care of myself.

"The way to get Aaron to do something is to tell him not to," my young mother was always saying. It was true. The idea that something was forbidden made it the greatest temptation of all.

When I was still pretty young, we visited my grandfather's pig farm. The adults issued several warnings not to touch the electric fence because "it will hurt you." In my mind, something worthy of so much attention begged to be tested. And I did with both hands. I had to be pried off that fence. My hands were badly burned.

More acute than any fear and pain I may have felt was a sense of gratification that I had learned the truth first-

not by chance

hand. Concrete proof was the motive of the born scientist and risk taker that I was.

I had the same attitude about pot. I determined I would try it the first chance I got, so that I'd have first-hand knowledge of its recreational effect. Drug use and ultimately abuse was not something into which I was peer pressured. I made a decision to experiment, almost scientifically, with drugs. When there was opportunity, I methodically tried pot, crack, coke, ecstasy and eventually snorted meth. I also was fairly thoughtful in my decision *not* to do heroine. The experimentation phase of drug use carried me through my tumultuous freshman year, the term in foster care and past high school.

Foster care didn't destroy me, nor did it transform me. While I enjoyed the stability, I was given a great deal of freedom. Even for a teenager, I behaved more like an adult. Independence had always been my best defense and it could be deceiving. For example, my foster parents allowed me to smoke, which would have been an easy habit to break had it been required.

Soon after I came to them, I took a job at Hardee's, a fast food joint, and worked for all my extras, including clothing. They also permitted me to be in WECEP — Work Experience Career Exploration Program. This took me away from school more hours and into the work force. I kept up on my schoolwork and worked as much as I could. Many years later, I found out that there was an allowance given to my foster parents that was to be passed on to me that I never saw. Additionally, my mother was

becoming a man

held responsible to pay back all of the expenses for my care.

In spite of the hidden inequities, I responded without bitterness to the positive expectations of young adulthood. Dave was the first real father that I ever had. And though they had never married, Dave and Kathy and their children were the closest example I had of a normal family. They treated me well — I had food and a decent house. In fact, I helped them build a house. Inheriting some more traditional father-son skills agreed with me.

One day when he took me fishing, Dave, my foster dad, reached into the cooler, grabbed a can of beer and popped the top. He looked at me thoughtfully for just a second before he said, "I know I'm not supposed to do this, but ya want a beer?"

He offered me the can. So we drank and talked and fished. The beer was no big deal to me, but the respect I sensed gave me a vague feeling of contentment and rest.

And if maturity is measured by demonstration of responsibility, I definitely qualified early. I took extra courses to get out of high school early. I attended only a few days out of my entire senior year in regular public high school, having already completed the needed credits to graduate. Then I began to take night courses at a local college, studying AutoCAD with plans of becoming an architect.

Foster care lasted almost two years before the courts decided that I could move in with my grandfather, a recent widower. I went to school morning and evening,

not by chance

worked 24 hours per week and served as primary caregiver for my grandfather. Cooking, cleaning, shopping and laundry — I did it all. Care giving and freedom did not erase the benefits of having him as a father figure in the most recent years of my life. He was kind and generous. The drunkenness that had triggered abuse in my mother's youth was long gone, and we shared a special bond.

Because of the heavy work and school schedule, I found myself using drugs only to get up or down as I needed.

During one visit, my mom found a stash of pot and attempted to ground me, but with all that I was doing with work and school, it was impossible for my grandfather to enforce. Basically, once I earned my driver's license, I was on my own.

Eat, drink and be merry. Find and satisfy your needs, and enjoy what physical pleasure you may come across. I operated in a concrete universe, living with two extremes. I worked hard in my jobs and pursued training for a good career. Finding out that I liked designing on paper, but not on the computer, prompted a change in direction from becoming an architect. I soon found out, however, that most architects used AutoCAD design programs. That meant computers. Ironically, I fell into the computer and communications industry, and I eventually landed a job with Cellular One.

The other extreme to working hard was playing hard. Getting high or having sex was the most pleasure a man could know, I imagined. Long ago, I had unplugged my

becoming a man

emotions, indulging at will in momentary diversions without guilt or concern. Surfing the net, I'd visit porn sites just because I was bored. I truly believed that good friends and good times were the best I could expect in life.

Many of my friends carried several pounds of tough history and had much the same philosophy about life as I did. Two of them were Stephanie and Jack. Oddly, Steph was married to one of my best buddies from high school, and they had a child. Jack was just sort of an easy-going rebel. Here I was part of another strange triad and together we made what turned out to be a life-changing decision.

Arizona had caught my eye when I vacationed there once. The Midwest was home, but I had grown restless, blaming it on the long winters of never-ending snow and subzero temperatures. A whim placed me interviewing for a job with AT&T during the same vacation. They gave me a kind of open-ended invitation to come and work. Weeks of sunshine would certainly be a pleasant alternative to weeks of snow.

I had a decent job back home though, and I didn't consider taking the job in Arizona very seriously at first.

"Man, you gotta do this," Jack started telling me as soon as he heard. "I'll go with ya. Let's just get out of this freakin' snow and start over."

Stephanie was looking to bale on her difficult married life.

Every time I saw them the next few weeks, they were making plans for us to get away.

not by chance

Ultimately, they persuaded me, and that spring, we headed for Arizona with everything the three of us owned stuffed into two cars. Each of us was running from something. Stephanie left a husband and child. Jack was running from responsibility. I was just running to run. None of us even told anyone we were leaving. We just left. It was two months before I talked to anyone back "home."

It had been several months since I had smoked anything, not even a joint. I was one week into training with AT&T, and I was relaxing in my new surroundings. Things were going pretty well, and Jack brought home some weed. I hesitated.

"Dude, you wanna celebrate your new job?" he hinted.

"Why not?" I thought, accepting the little roll of marijuana. It was already lit. I took a long drag and handed it back to him. "Thanks."

The next day when I arrived at training, we were given a surprise drug test. Of course, I failed. And lost the job.

I would spend the next two months looking for work. Without finding it, I soon plunged toward financial ruin. I missed several bills and lost the nearly perfect credit rating I'd established at the age of 20 before running away to Arizona.

At least I had a place to live. I had moved in with Stephanie's husband's cousin, Daniel, whom I'd met while on vacation. Finally, I did find work. I also found out that had I not left, I would have been promoted to Cell Site Technician with Cellular One, with a $50,000 annual salary and a company Jeep.

becoming a man

I really regretted some of my choices I'd made now that I was suffering the consequences. But the depression I felt over the cost took me not away from drugs, but deeper into them.

I met Linda at work. She reminded me of my high school sweetheart. She had brown hair and eyes, a petite frame and the same sense of humor. Back in high school, Tanya and I had met in study hall, passing messages on a notepad since we weren't allowed to talk. Once we officially got together, we were together for three and a half years and planned to marry someday. We drifted apart when we moved in different directions, me to Minneapolis and she to Green Bay, a year after graduation. It had been very hard for me to admit the end of the relationship.

Linda and I became friends when we hit it off at work. Very simply, I liked her. We started seeing each other at other times outside of work. This time was limited as she had three children from her first marriage. Every other weekend, though, the kids were with their dad and so we'd spend that time together. It wasn't long before we were regularly dabbling in meth together. Although she had drifted from her more stable upbringing, she gave our friendship more real strength, while I moved without resistance into care giving.

A few months before we had moved in together, I arrived home to find my roommate's friend raping Linda as she was passed-out drunk. My roommate and long-time friend, Jack, stood by, doing nothing. Not long after that, Linda and I were married. Within a year, we were sepa-

not by chance

rated but got back together in another year out of misunderstood emptiness we felt as need for each other.

Each time I had tried a different drug it was a conscious decision. From my experience, I would form my opinion about whether I would like to try it again in the future. Though I liked most of them, I was not compelled to seek them out. Most often, I used when the occasion presented itself.

"You should try smoking it," a friend of a friend of a friend I met suggested about meth. "It's way more powerful than snorting."

He introduced me to a test-tube-like pipe with a bubble on one end and taught me how to measure and heat the crystal substance in the bowl. Skillfully, he turned the tube gently, and I saw a vapor forming and drifting up the tube. I followed his lead and inhaled the vapor. Immediately, I felt a rush of adrenaline like never before. The high that followed was beyond description. This was the first drug, perhaps the only drug, which I'd never walk away from.

For the next five years, my life would virtually revolve around this chemistry. Meth energized and enabled me to perform highly repetitive activities and absorb volumes of information. Under its influence, my brain was convinced that all my physical needs were met. I'd go days without eating or sleeping.

Linda gave up trying to bring me home. We had a precious little daughter together, Ariana. Linda's maternal instincts kicked in and motivated her to pursue a better

becoming a man

life for her and the children. While she may have loved me when we married, I'd been somewhat disconnected. At the time, getting married seemed like the right thing to do for her, for me and to please her parents. I felt like a miserable failure at it. The shame drove me even farther away.

She was drawn to church for comfort and guidance. There was a church group called Two Rivers that she especially liked and wanted me to come and visit.

"I think you'd like the people," she said. "They're from Wisconsin."

I had to admit, it was nice to hear Midwestern accents and to explore things in common. But I did not buy the religious stuff whatsoever.

"Let's get together sometime," Pastor Tom invited.

For some reason, I agreed to meet with him. Even though I was sporadic at church, I couldn't imagine his motives.

Week after week, he took me out to lunch, and we would debate the scientific foundation of the Bible. His knowledge of it, ability to quote huge passages and patience as he explained how they refuted my lack of faith was amazing. But I was more amazed that he would spend so much time with a loser like me, when I clearly was not into what he was telling me.

"What about all these other faiths?" I would ask. "How can you say that this one version is the absolute truth?"

"Because it is, Aaron, and someday you will see that."

"If there is only one true God, then prove it." I threw that out when I could no longer handle the relational

not by chance

proof that was sitting right across the booth from me in a restaurant.

I spiraled deeper and deeper. Nothing but skin and bones, 5'7" and 115 pounds, I kept a manic pace with work. I was up 24/7 working to support my family, and meth is what enabled me to do it. I'd gone almost a month without eating anything but a handful of packages of Ramen noodles. There were periods where I was nearly psychotic from sleep deprivation. All but six of my teeth were damaged or ruined.

Paranoia overtook me. It's common for meth users. I still convinced myself I was different, but I was no less a thief and an addict than the pathetic company I kept.

One friend had equipped his house so well that he had a closed circuit TV mounted so that we could see anyone approaching the house, notably police or dissatisfied dealers. I was spinning pretty good one time and looked up at the monitor to see my wife coming up the sidewalk with Ariana beside her. In dismay, she shook her head and asked my daughter, "Oh, dear, what is Daddy doing now? What's Daddy doing now?"

Indignant, I asked her about it later.

"No, I was never there. I'm not coming to get you anymore. I wouldn't bring Ariana anyway, you know that," Linda swore.

"Aaron? Aaron? C'mon now. It's okay, buddy. Can you hear me?" Someone was saying my name.

Opening my eyes, I saw Pastor Tom leaning over me. I panicked.

becoming a man

Oh, God. I passed out, and he's found me in the hideout. I sat upright, ready to spring and run.

But he chuckled, "Whoa, now, you might be a little wobbly. How ya feelin' there, friend?"

I looked around and saw I wasn't in a drug house. I was home, and Pastor Tom was kneeling beside me. Running my hand through my hair, I relaxed a little and leaned my head on my arms, which were folded around my up drawn knees.

The pastor was still kneeling in front of me but sat back on his heels with his hands on his knees, awaiting an answer to his question.

"Man, what happened?" I looked at him sideways, still resting my head on my arm. I felt different, a little weak, but my head was clearing and feelings I hadn't known before started to engulf my senses.

"What do you think happened?" he asked. His voice held both kindness and joy.

"You put your hand on my head and prayed. That's the last thing I remember. What happened? I must have passed out. Why?" Still sitting on the floor, I had no idea how I'd come to be flat on my back minutes before. "How long was I out?"

"Well, Aaron, it's been about 30 or 45 minutes, I'd guess," he began. He helped me to my feet, and we sat on opposite ends of the couch. "I wish that I had a video camera so that you could see what happened. When I began to pray for you, your eyes rolled back in your head, and there were two or three other entities that began to talk through

not by chance

you. I cast them out in the name of Jesus. Do you notice anything different?"

I felt completely different.

"You mean entities, like demons?"

"That is what I'd call them. I think you'll be glad they're gone."

I had to admit I was beginning to feel pretty good. An hour earlier, I would have argued that I didn't believe in demons. The agnostic would have demanded he produce a videotape or eyewitnesses to this "exorcism." But I was not the same person. What I was feeling now was so powerful and real and so different than anything else I had ever experienced in my life. Something inside me said, "He is telling the truth."

"I guess I really do feel a difference," I conceded aloud. "I feel lighter, physically and emotionally."

I had challenged him to prove to me that there is a God. Now he had. I began to believe because I could no longer not believe.

I stayed clean and sober for about six or eight months after that. It was the right thing to do, I thought, because I had confessed belief in God. I'd converted. It was a feeble attempt to get my act together. I maintained a number of reckless connections.

Sean had been a good friend for several years since I'd first moved to Arizona. We shared an interest in computers. And in drugs. Buying a computer through him gave me an excuse to visit one last time before getting down to business with rehab. The scientist in me believed

becoming a man

in several things I hadn't before, but the addict had not yet met Jesus.

Nor had the husband. Frankly, the only reason I'd agreed to the whole rehab thing was because Linda was at the end of her rope.

"I'm done with you," she'd said. "I can't live this way."

We were at an impasse, and although I was interested in being a Christian, I didn't fully understand it. I was going through the motions. My commitment to Christ was more a mental surrender to the possibility that God could help me than whole-hearted dedication of my life to him. My dependency was still on myself, my brains and a variety of chemicals, both legal and illegal. None of these factors were improving the marriage. We had married too young and for the wrong reasons. Although I felt affection toward my wife, motivation to save the marriage was limited. Reversing the damage was just not humanly possible.

Pastor Tom hooked me up with a program called Teen Challenge. It offered me a year away from my life to study the Bible. Being away from the drug scene couldn't hurt, I figured. I'd just lost the best job I'd ever had for "no call, no show," and needed to sort things out. So I'd agreed to the 13-month program. I was still experimenting with God, and that sort of justified one last dance with the devil.

I am going to go out and get really messed up one last time. Then I'll never do it again. Ever. Deep down, I truly meant it. I had no idea, though, of the claim God had taken in my life because I'd given him just a little room.

not by chance

Half-heartedly, I tried to talk myself into doing the right thing as I headed toward Sean's door. "Just get the computer and get out. Need to be home before Linda."

The house looked older than it was. It stood on a stark lot a little further back than the others on the street. Shades on the windows that faced the street were permanently drawn shut. The inhabitants, most of whose names did not appear on the lease agreement, did not care for the light or the exposure of their activities. The whole unhappy place seemed to turn away from the street in shame and secrecy because the door that faced the side where the driveway laid was the worse for wear. An overgrown hedge actually bordered the sidewalk and street and obscured the activities that took place within its bounds. It was obvious, though, by the traffic in and out, day and night, that this was a drug house. Only those who wanted to be deceived or didn't care could deny it.

I stepped over the threshold and into a horrible void that sucked all will from inside of me and crushed me from the outside. In this vacuum, day one turned into day four. I was probably on my third or fourth hit in the past couple of days, and I had plenty left. The faces around me had mixed and changed several times. I had finally taken a seat in a tired-looking easy chair near the window. I liked to be by a window to see who might be coming. But there had been so much coming and going that I grew more paranoid of those inside than those outside the house. Sean was gone. An unspecified warning sounded in my head, or maybe it was in my heart. Nothing was normal.

becoming a man

In fact, everything felt horribly wrong. I pushed the thought from my mind and gave all my attention to a familiar ritual.

I picked up the clear tube and tapped a portion of "ice" into the bubbled end of the tube. Carefully, I warmed the bowl with my lighter. Watching the vapor curl up the tube as solid turned to liquid and liquid to gas, I expertly turned the tube back and forth to maintain the pattern of heating and cooling to produce the vapor. That was enough to raise my expectations. When there were several perfect ribbons spiraling up the tube in response to my twisting it, I inhaled deeply as I had hundreds of times in the past five years, anticipating the unequalled rush I'd come to depend upon. At any moment, I knew I would be spinning. I closed my eyes and lay my head back, but it seemed to be taking longer than usual.

Suddenly, my hair stood on end, and a tingling sensation like electricity pulsed through my body. I immediately recognized the sensation as the Holy Spirit, because this is what I'd felt in church. But this was not church. Why and how would God be here in this drug house? With me?

"Stop!" I froze as though the voice was audible and loud. It was neither. It was firm but quiet, speaking somehow from inside of me, but it wasn't me.

Looking around, I recognized to my dread that I had abandoned myself to this miserable existence. Something within was telling me I didn't belong here. At the very same moment, I realized I was stone cold sober. Never had

not by chance

I come face to face with myself like this.

"I've got to get out … something is terribly wrong. I've got to get out." An alarm was going off inside.

I looked down at the pile of meth I just purchased and the paraphernalia in the chair beside me. All of a sudden, it was like liquid mercury. I'd been protecting it, but now I had to get rid of it.

At the same moment, something new and indescribable was forming at the core of my being. It wasn't just a feeling, it was a knowing. Beyond belief, it was a rock-hard conviction. "You don't have to do this anymore. This is not you."

Instantly, I stood up. I gathered together the leftover bags of crystal meth, the tube and the lighter. A guy who'd been hanging out for a day or two, getting high, yelled some obscenity as he eyed me grabbing my stuff. Protectively, he rolled into a defensive position around his stash on the floor in the corner. He'd forgotten about the stolen CDs he'd been hiding under his jacket, and they clattered out where everyone could see. When the owner saw them, he dove across the room to exact justice, lifting the thief to his feet and against the wall in one abusive motion. They began a fight to the death, screaming, punching, kicking and swearing.

"Leave," the inner voice gently reminded me.

My heart beating wildly, I did what I never could have done on my own, what no meth addict can do. I set my entire drug stash aside on the coffee table and fled.

I placed my hand on the receiver of the phone in the

becoming a man

booth of the Quick Trip store down the street. Panting from the effort of running three blocks and from a new rush of God's amazing deliverance, I leaned my head against my upraised arm. My other hand shook as it dug for the coins, shoved them into the slot and pushed the buttons of our home phone number.

"Hello?" Linda sounded tired, dejected.

"Hey." I knew she'd know my voice, and I wanted to explain everything before she hung up. When I started to speak, though, I choked. There was silence, and I longed just to hear her voice.

"Something has happened," I managed to say, with waves of new emotions flooding over me. "Can you come pick me up?"

"Oh, Aaron." I could tell she was going to turn me down. Remorse filled me.

"Linda, listen, I'm telling you — I'm totally sober. I want to come home and talk." It was still hard to breathe, and I felt like crying. I made an impatient circle in the tiny space and found that the stiff cord of the pay phone yanked me to a stop.

Turning back toward the phone, I leaned my free hand against the phone again. "Please," I pled desperately, gripping the receiver with my other hand.

"If I come to get you, will you get in the car?" Her response was laced with suspicion but not accusation. She had tried many times to get me home when I'd been somewhere getting high. I felt the weight of her disappointment and couldn't blame her for doubting me.

not by chance

"Yes, I promise." It sounded lame, but it was all that I could say.

"All right, where are you?"

God slipped into the tiny opening I had given him. That was something I never expected. Having forced the issue of concrete, physical evidence, my expectations were very limited. Not only did he prove himself, he revealed himself miraculously by bringing to life something that was dead — my spirit. All I had known in my life was physical survival and pleasure. The new man that I have become is not controlled by that part of himself. Areas that had been exposed to the enemy, whether voluntarily or involuntarily, changed instantly when exposed in the tiniest way to Jesus.

I was four days overdue checking in at Teen Challenge. Residents are required to empty their pockets when they check in. I turned over my cigarettes, lighter and money. I was given a room assignment, bedding, a schedule and a mentor.

I promised myself, my wife and my family that I would give 100 percent to the program. It was a good program based on the Bible. I knew it was really going to make a difference. My mentor was another pastor that I found was easy to talk to. He prayed with me each morning and encouraged me in the studies. I adapted to the structured schedule and the somewhat restricted environment surprisingly well. Something was nagging at my spirit, though. At first, I was afraid to mention it. *They'll think I just want to get out of here so I can go back to the drugs.*

becoming a man

I wanted to go home.

"You need to finish the program," I told myself. "You promised Linda."

A week went by, and the homesickness grew.

This is ridiculous, I told myself. *I never felt this strongly about my wife and kids when I was off doing drugs.*

But I was no longer an addict. I was a child of God, a husband and a father. A new kind of love was growing in my heart, and I couldn't dismiss the idea that I needed to be home supporting her.

It hasn't been long enough. You need to honor the 13 months.

I mentioned this to my mentor, asking him how to know whether it was my desire or the Lord's. He prayed with me.

After two weeks, I couldn't stand it any longer. "George, I really think I need to go home."

"Aaron, we aren't going to force you to stay," he said.

I waited for him to say "*But...*" and try to talk me out of it.

Instead, he encouraged me to pray and seek the Lord and gave me his word that he'd be praying, too. I returned to my room and asked God to direct me. When I closed my eyes and said, "Jesus," all I could think about was my wife and kids.

Nervously, I went back to George. "I think I am supposed to go home."

He told me to go sign myself out of the program. He

not by chance

released me without argument.

I had no money and no car. I packed up my few items of clothing, my Bible and personal items. With about 80 pounds on my back, I left on foot. I walked close to 15 miles before someone happened along to give me a bus ticket, but I could have walked another 15 and not felt the pack on my back or blisters on my feet.

The caller ID told Linda the call she got at work was from home. It would not have been unusual for my stepchildren, Jeremy, Myriah, Allison or even Ariana to need something, but she did not expect my voice. When I heard her voice, I cried.

"If anyone is in Christ, he is a new creation; old things have passed away; behold, all things have become new."

I cannot say that my dead marriage was restored. Instead, it was resurrected and made new, like me. The love I began to feel for Linda, Ariana and even my stepchildren was brand new, like no other feeling I've ever had. It continues to grow. Honoring the period of separation that would have accompanied my stay in Teen Challenge, I moved into my own place, allowing my wife and children time to process the changes God was making. I would see them more frequently and be available to learn to be a real husband and father.

Although I didn't graduate from the Teen Challenge program, God completely delivered me from addiction to drugs and even cigarettes.

And this new Aaron is now a father again.

fear failed
the story of aimee ghimire
written by arlene knickerbocker

I grew up with a powerful enemy who wore many faces. He visited me day and night. His name was "Terror."

Terror introduced himself to me one night when I was 4 years old. I smelled Daddy's aftershave and noticed both he and Mama were in their good clothes. I heard Daddy tell my brother from outside my door to take a good message if someone called. I felt a heaviness come over me.

"Are you going away, Mama?" I asked when my mother tucked me into bed.

She evaded my question and whispered close to my ear, "Go to sleep, little one. I'll see you in the morning." She smiled and pulled the covers around my neck, being sure to slip her fingers between the sheets and the mattress to provide an extra safe fit. She then turned off the lights and exited the room.

As I heard her soft voice whisper to Daddy in the hallway, sudden fear raced through my chest, and I leapt from my bed and sprinted to the hallway, where I clung to my parents for dear life.

My yellow room, with its vivid print bedspread and curtains, seemed bright and cheery when Mama and Daddy were home and the sun shone, but it was dark and scary at night.

not by chance

"Please, don't go. Please."

"We have to go, Aimee." She peeled my arms from her legs. "Go to the basement room where your older brothers are. They will take care of you."

I lived in Vienna, Austria, with my missionary parents. I had been to "meetings" with them at various churches, where they stood up in front and spoke to a lot of people. I knew people were depending on them to speak that night. Fear clung to me, as I had clung to my mother — but because of my training, I obeyed.

Terror became bolder each time my parents went away. One evening, my parents were late returning from another meeting, and the usual fear came over me. Then it escalated until I threw myself on the bed and cried, "They're dead! They're dead!" I put a pillow over my head, and only God heard my cries. I remained in my room alone, while my dark adversary manipulated my imagination. Ugly scenarios of their deaths bombarded my brain. I saw a car cross the yellow median line and crash into them. Their bloody bodies flew from the vehicle and lay lifeless on the pavement. I went into what I know now as a panic attack, but my brothers in the next room never knew.

Even if no real threat existed, my body responded as if I lived in terrible peril. I spent many nights cowering by a window in my room, sobbing, shaking and biting my nails until they bled. My heart pounded so hard that my sweat-soaked nightgown moved with it. I felt sick to my stomach. I kept watching out that window, my eyes glued to the

fear failed

driveway, waiting for the headlights, until I saw our car turn in.

Fear ruled my life, even when I wasn't experiencing panic attacks. Fear of disappointing my parents caused me to obey. Fear of what people might think directed my actions. Fear gripped me and wouldn't let go when I felt a loss of control or when I experienced separation from my parents.

Generally, I kept a happy face for people to see. Nobody knew the battles I fought or the scars they left. One day, when I was 10 years old, however, fear drove me to seek comfort.

Mama was gone, and Daddy was in the house studying. I realized that she had been out shopping quite a long time, and then the fear set in. Heat climbed up my back, and anxiety tightened my muscles until my head ached. I climbed a tree and sat in it, crying and watching for my mom to drive up our road. After an hour or so, fear drove me down from the tree and into the house. My father looked startled as I ran crying into the room.

"I'm scared Mama won't come home," I bellowed into his shoulder. "I think Mama might die!"

I had finally uttered my fearful words aloud to another person. This was a big step for me. I fell into my dad's arms, exhausted.

"There, there. It's okay." He patted my back as he ran his fingers through my hair.

"But I'm afraid she has been in a crash."

not by chance

"She'll come home," he soothed me. I laid my head in his lap while he stroked my hair and repeated, "She's okay. Everything's okay."

I appreciated his loving kindness, but nothing felt okay until Mom came home alive.

That was just the beginning.

Terror had moved into my life and brought all of its baggage. When I was 15, we traveled from Austria to visit family in Houston, Texas. One hot, humid day, I fell ill. Soon an internal alarm sounded in my mind, and I couldn't help but think, *Oh no, I'm going to die. Why me, God? Why now?*

I tried to deal with the fear alone as I often did, but finally, I went into the kitchen where my mother was working.

"Mom, I'm sick."

She felt my head. "I don't think you have a fever. You'll be all right." She gave me a drink of water and patted my shoulder. Then she turned back to her long list of chores.

I wanted to tell her, "But I'm dying." However, my compassion for her won. *Raising five kids and being a missionary is more than enough. I don't want to add to her load.* I walked out of the room and faced my fright alone.

Dread grew heavier, and I grew weaker. This confirmed my fears. One day, we went to the YMCA where my two younger brothers played basketball. I watched and unnerving thoughts started taking over my mind. *They are*

fear failed

having so much fun. It isn't fair that I am sick and dying. I'll never see them grow up. I pictured myself in a casket being lowered into the ground, while my family stood nearby, weeping.

I felt nausea and weakness for three days. During that time, I mentally said goodbye to each member of my family and waited to die.

When I started feeling better and realized I was going to live, I prayed, "Thank you, God, for giving me another chance at life." I thought I'd beaten my fear of death, but it kept reviving.

***

Daddy had piles of books in the room where he studied. One day, I walked in and started looking at various titles. One caught my eye. I cleared my throat to get Dad's attention and asked, "May I read this book?"

"Certainly. Just put it back when you're done." Then he looked at the title and noted, "You've chosen well."

He was right. *Practicing the Presence of God* by Brother Lawrence inspired me. All the Bible knowledge I had gained became real to me.

I had gone to Sunday school and church all of my life. When I was 3 years old, I realized I couldn't be "good enough" to get into heaven. The Sunday school teacher talked about how Jesus had taken my punishment, and I should accept his gift and tell him thank you. She called this "accepting Jesus as your Savior." I had prayed with

not by chance

her. I felt bad that Jesus had to die because I did wrong things. I kept telling him I was sorry.

After reading this book, though, I moved to a new level. Instead of focusing on my behavior, I began to develop a personal relationship with God. I literally felt as if God walked with me all the time. I don't feel like self-doubt necessarily came over me. This same sense of his presence did come and go over the years in smaller versions, but not often and not for long. My heart wanted the Lord, but I was thrown off by fear, worry, depression and then the world.

"God, please help me," I prayed.

I turned in the Bible to Psalm 46:1, "God is our refuge and strength, an ever-present help in trouble." However, I didn't know how to draw on his strength. I didn't feel his presence anymore. *Where are you, God?* I would cry at night. *I can't feel anything.*

I read, "Don't worry about anything; instead, pray about everything." (Philippians 4:6a) Then I felt guilty and worried more. *I'm not supposed to worry*, I told myself. The more I tried not to worry, the more I focused on it, and the more I worried.

***

Years passed — years peppered by anxiety attacks and fear. It was time for me to go away from my parents. Up until now, they had gone away from me from time to time. Now I was the one leaving. I packed everything from my

fear failed

drawers and closet, took one last look around the bedroom that had been my haven for years and hugged my parents.

"Goodbye. Remember we love you. Be good at college," they whispered, as they hugged me at the security checkpoint. Streams of tears stained my face as sadness swept my body. I would be so far away — what would this new life be like?

It was a long trip from Austria to Washington State. We had traveled often throughout my childhood, and I never minded airplane trips. Now, however, I experienced waves of panic. *I'll die on this airplane and never attend college. I'll never get married and have kids,* I thought.

"What's wrong?" my seatmate asked, staring at my hands that were clutching the seat until my knuckles turned white.

"Nothing." I smiled and tried to relax my hands, while I wondered if I might have a heart attack.

The flying phobia continued every time I flew, and I prepared for death repeatedly. Each time I left my apartment, I left it ready for someone to clear out easily in case I never returned. *I don't want anyone to find my apartment messy and think less of me. I'll need to clean the kitchen and make sure everything is in its place.* I threw away any notes or anything I didn't want others to see.

Each time I came back safely, I thanked God profusely for giving me another chance.

About that time, I met a man named Shailesh at college. He seemed to have the stability I lacked. He fasci-

not by chance

nated me, challenged me and entertained me. We became good friends, and eventually realized we were in love. Our relationship faced problems, though.

In my senior year, I faced more than occasional panic attacks. A heavy, dark cloud descended on me. I prayed, "Where are you, God? Why do I feel so dark inside?"

Shailesh and I clung to each other, yet our differences made us think our relationship could never last. I needed time and space to figure out what I believed and if Shailesh and I should continue our relationship.

I continued to pray but received only silence from God.

"Life is meaningless," I cried. The gray haze of depression colored the way I saw everything, like wearing a pair of dark glasses made from someone else's prescription.

***

After I graduated from college, I moved to Japan to teach English. My depression spiraled downward. In the daytime, I went through the motions of normal living.

"Hi, want to go somewhere tonight?" various acquaintances called to ask.

"No, thanks. I have a lot to do," I would answer. Then I turned on the television and ate sweets to the point of nausea. I often escaped through sexual fantasies. When I shut off the distractions, fear came to call. Sometimes I covered my head and gave into the trepidation. Sometimes I repeated, "Jesus, Jesus," until I fell asleep.

fear failed

Shailesh and I had an off-again, on-again relationship. He was living in Wisconsin, while I was in Japan. We kept in touch; after a time, I moved near him to see if things might work out between us. We attended church together, and everything seemed fine on the surface. However, the dangerous undercurrent of fear and depression remained. I found myself crying during the services.

"What's wrong?" Shailesh kept asking.

I always had the same answer: "Nothing. Leave me alone."

Actually, the depression wasn't the whole reason for my crying. God was speaking to me again. I still felt empty and needy, but for the first time in several years, a glimmer of hope was in sight.

I was teaching English part-time and looking for a second job when I received a phone call that changed my life.

"Hi, you were referred to us. Would you be able to come for an interview this week? We have a fantastic opportunity to offer you," said the woman on the other end of the line.

"That sounds good," I replied enthusiastically. "I've been looking for a second job."

At the time, I thought God was answering prayer. I had mentioned my job search to a few friends, but I wasn't sure who would have referred me.

"Oh, you could add this position easily. It requires very few hours and pays big money." As the lady's words reverberated in the back of my brain, I started to think of things I could do with the extra money — good things —

not by chance

things that would help others, like starting an orphanage in another country.

I went to the interview the next day. Impeccably dressed people sat in the plush waiting room. Classical music played in the background. It all seemed quite impressive.

"You have been specially selected for this tremendous position. Will you please follow me into our seminar room? We have a video you have to see." In the video, we saw person after person testify about how much money he or she made with little effort.

I fell for their lies. How ironic that I struggled to trust God, but I trusted these unworthy strangers. I invested nearly all the money I had (actually, more than I had). I even borrowed money from Shailesh. I followed their suggestions exactly. I made hundreds of calls like the one that had drawn me into the business. I lied to the people, saying someone had referred them. I rationalized my actions by telling myself, *it doesn't matter. Nobody cares what I tell the people I call, as long as I can recruit them and earn more money. After all, I am letting them know about a great opportunity.*

This began to affect my relationship with Shailesh. We had several blowout fights, and many of them ended with him yelling and me crying.

"Are you working again tomorrow?" Shailesh asked one weekend. "We never see each other anymore. We have to have a serious talk."

fear failed

"You don't understand. Finally, I'm excited about something. I'm opening my own office soon," I told him with confidence. What I didn't tell him was the busy work made it possible for me to push my life's fears and depression aside temporarily. When I didn't have goals to focus on, my fears returned. Sometimes graphic images of death attacked my mind, but I had experienced this since childhood and never discussed it with others. I thought everybody went through the same thing. I hated my evil companion, but living with him seemed normal to me.

Depression entrenched itself even deeper into my soul, while visions of wealth and fame spurred me to work harder. *Maybe if I get out of this money trap, I will feel happy.* Since I had invested all of my money, I felt tremendous pressure to succeed. My superiors stressed how important it was to dress for success, so I maxed out my credit cards buying expensive clothing and other things I thought would help me find success — and fulfillment.

Then the bottom dropped out of my life. The Internal Revenue Service audited my tax records and found I had claimed expenses that were not eligible. I left the business, and soon it was shut down for illegal practices, such as false advertising. The man I rented my office from sued me for non-payment.

About that time, I met a missionary. Talking with him reminded me of the deep craving in my heart to serve God, like my parents. I realized how far I had moved from my teenage experience of walking closely with God.

not by chance

I knew Shailesh was waiting to talk with me. Finally, I called him. When he said, "Hello," his familiar voice sounded strong. *I wish I had his strength*, I thought.

"You were right. We need to have a serious talk," I said. "Can you come over tonight?"

When he came to the door, he looked even more serious than usual. His brow had deep creases I hadn't seen before. In the course of our conversation, I told him, "I can't deny the desire to serve God that lies buried deep in my heart. Though I haven't been following him, God is still wooing me. Do you understand?"

"I knew you weren't giving yourself to me all the way. I've always felt that I love you more than you love me. I've always given myself to you more than you have given yourself to me. I think our relationship is going nowhere," he replied with disappointment.

"I'm sorry, Shailesh, I want to love you fully. I'm so confused." I glanced up at the man I had become so close to over the last few years, hoping he could understand but seeing in his eyes that this wasn't something he could be content with.

"I'm sorry, too, Aimee. I don't want to continue with our relationship, unless you can love me the way I love you."

We agreed to break up, which hurt more than I had expected. It drove me to distractions, rather than to God. I still taught English to foreign students, and soon, I began partying with them. One young student from the Middle

fear failed

East enticed me, and he manipulated me. We began a relationship, of sorts, and I noticed myself changing.

A friend noted, "All you talk about anymore is entertainment and sexual pleasure."

"Well, I'm going to see my family for Christmas this week. There won't be any fun there," I joked. I thought I was getting good at acting out my double life. During my visit, I tried to act like my old outgoing self, but I didn't succeed. One night, I started weeping at the dinner table. The more I tried to stop, the worse it became. I fell apart.

"What's wrong?" both my parents asked.

"I miss Shailesh."

I wanted to tell them everything, but I also wanted them to think highly of me. I felt angry the whole time I was home, and I couldn't understand it. I felt angry toward them, angry toward my circumstances and angry at myself because I couldn't control what was going on inside me and around me.

When I went back to my apartment, I took a cold heart with me. Alcohol is a depressant, and I didn't need that — but I craved the escape it offered. Life seemed meaningless, bland and sad. Fear had invaded my life. Then depression took over, while fear popped in and out. Now confusion was barging into the picture. *Am I going insane?* I wondered.

I knew I needed a miracle. I still attended church, but I had neglected my relationship with God until I didn't apply anything I learned at church to my life at all. Around people, I acted courageous and strong. I told nobody

not by chance

about the ferocious battle going on inside. Instead, I just kept medicating myself with alcohol, sexual pleasure and other distractions.

***

One day, Shailesh knocked on my apartment door. The second I saw him I knew something was different. Usually somber, his eyes beamed, and he was all smiles.

"May I come in?"

"Sure," I replied. "I'm just putting something in the oven. Come on in the kitchen."

He sat at my little corner table and dropped a bombshell.

"I have to tell you something," he started slowly. "I've become a follower of Jesus, and God spoke to me."

I stared at him, not knowing what to say.

"He told me you're going to be my wife."

I didn't know how to respond. My thoughts ran wild. *It's not fair!* I cried in my head. *Why don't you speak to me, God?* I was so deep in misery, I couldn't be happy for Shailesh, and I didn't feel any love toward him. I sat in silence.

"Well, I'm leaving now, but I'll keep praying about us." He started to kiss me, but I turned my head.

A few months later, Shailesh showed up again. By then, I had broken things off with my Middle Eastern student. I was ready to have the small flame of hope inside me fanned into a fire.

fear failed

Shailesh looked up at me.

"I'm willing to see if our relationship can work. But I can't do this unless you can give your heart to me completely."

I couldn't promise that. Wiping tears away, I answered, "Can you give me some time?"

"Okay, but only because I know God spoke to me."

I knew I had to do something drastic. I fasted for five days, just drinking liquids. I stayed in pajamas or sweats. It was early January, and I was on school break, and I sat on my bed cross-legged, staring out the window at the snow-covered trees for hours at a time. I drank hot tea and cried hot tears. I read the Bible, and on the fifth day, several verses in Jeremiah pierced my heart. Then I started reading Isaiah, chapter 30. The first verse says, "'Woe to the obstinate children,' declares the Lord, 'to those who carry out plans that are not mine.'" Verse 15 says, "This is what the sovereign Lord, the holy one of Israel, says: 'In repentance and rest is your salvation, in quietness and trust is your strength, but you would have none of it.'"

The rest of the chapter tells how God rescued the Israelites from slavery, but they wanted to go back to Egypt. I realized God had rescued me from pride and rebellion, too. Then I had gone back to its slavery.

At this point, I saw a stunning and life-changing vision. I saw a bright path before me. An illuminated cross rose high at the end, shining its light over Shailesh, who stood in the path. I was in a dark place where huge, locked gates with thick iron bars surrounded me. Somehow, I

not by chance

knew one gate stood for wealth, another for sexual pleasure, another for reputation, another for gluttony and another for entertainment. These gates looked enticing and exciting. I saw my hands clamoring for treasures behind these gates.

I knew exactly what God was telling me. I had spent the past years seeking fulfillment from wealth, sexual pleasure, prestige, gluttony and fun. I had worshipped these counterfeit gods, while ignoring the true and living God who could have given me the fulfillment and joy I longed to attain. I knew I stood at a crossroad.

I lived in an old apartment building with wooden floors and a throw rug by my bed. I slid out of bed, knelt on that little rug and prayed. "God, please release me; set me free. I am so desperate. Break me out of this prison of lies. I don't want to be selfish anymore. I want to be free. Kill the old me, who is full of fear, rebellion, hate and lust for things of this world.

"The wonderful things you created have become my idols. I've been serving creation rather than you, the Creator. I've been looking to them for satisfaction, when only you can satisfy. I am here before you, empty — ready for you to fill me with new life. I want to receive your forgiveness, your cleansing."

I felt Jesus accept me at that time. He became my life — my everything. He saved me from my desperation. He became my Lord, my master.

The moment I turned from my life of bad choices to follow God, his spirit touched me. Suddenly, the gray haze

fear failed

lifted. The world filled with color. My sadness, confusion, depression and darkness all disappeared. It was as if I entered a new world full of smiles, joy and fulfillment.

"My Lord, I don't know words that can express my thanks. You have calmed me and stilled my soul. Everything around me is colorful, beautiful. You are eternal peace."

Immediately, I thought, *I have to call Shailesh.* When he answered, my heart leaped. "Can you come over here right now?" I asked.

"Yes," he answered. Without knowing any more, he dropped everything and came to my apartment immediately.

As soon as I greeted him, I told him about my experience, and I ended with, "I know I'm supposed to marry you. My heart overflows with love for you."

He responded with a kiss. We made a life-long commitment to each other that day, and we were officially engaged within three months.

***

My circumstances were nearly perfect — I had an amazing guy and an amazing God — but I still dealt with bouts of fear. One afternoon, I felt God leading me to a prayer room in our city. There, a man approached me and told me he had a message for me from the Lord.

"The Lord says, 'I love you very much,'" he said to me. "I am getting you ready. You were in a trap of the devil,

not by chance

but I will use this as a testimony. Shailesh and you are at the same place and are on this journey together. He needs much love. Love will bring him healing and will bring you both out of your prison. Perfect love casts out all fear. I have a higher vision for you. I am blessing your union."

I never saw the man who delivered God's message before or since that day.

Among others, the Bible verse he referred to has become real to me. "There is no room in love for fear. Well-formed [perfect] love banishes fear. Since fear is crippling, a fearful life — fear of death, fear of judgment — is one not yet fully formed in love." (1 John 4:18 The Message)

Shailesh and I started attending a new church called Lake City Church in Madison, Wisconsin. We needed a new start to our new life. One day, I realized I still needed cleansing in my spirit and soul. Although peace lived in my soul most of the time now, panic still visited me on occasion. We heard about Theophostic Prayer Ministry, and I went there seeking prayer. A minister prayed with me and asked me to face my disturbing memories. I closed my eyes, and a demon of fear appeared. I actually saw it with my spiritual eyes. I felt sick to my stomach and weak.

Next, I pictured myself in the womb. Soon the picture changed to my mother and then to her mother, my maternal grandmother. Later my mother told me she had fallen into a deep depression and feared dying while she was pregnant with me. She never experienced this at any other time in her life.

fear failed

"Spirit of fear, come out of Aimee, in the name of Jesus Christ," the minister commanded.

The knot in my stomach and feeling of doom left immediately. In its place, peace entered. A voice that I know was the Lord spoke to me, "My arms are around you." This phrase kept repeating in my mind.

A few days later, I read in the Bible, "The eternal God is your refuge, and his everlasting arms are under you. He thrusts out the enemy before you; it is he who cries, 'Destroy them.'" (Deuteronomy 33:27)

I thought fear had fled for good, but some time later, I felt oppression again. A pastor visiting from India spoke one night, and somehow, he touched me.

"You're trembling," Shailesh whispered.

"I know. I can't help it," I replied, shaking.

Shailesh encouraged me to talk to the pastor after the meeting. It was an intense time.

"Let's go," Shailesh encouraged. I pushed him away, but eventually, I went with him into another room.

I sat in a chair with three pastors around me and Shailesh next to me. One pastor named demons of death, suicide, depression, self-accusation and anxiety that he saw living inside of me.

"Oh, there are so many," I whispered.

"No, that is a lie from the demons. They want to appear formidable to you," the pastor said.

The three pastors agreed and told the demons, "In the name of Jesus, we command you to go and not return."

not by chance

I wept and doubled over with nausea. I knew I was in the midst of a violent spiritual battle. The pastors kept praying, and suddenly, I felt the spirits leave with a "whoosh." They have never returned.

One of the pastors assured me, "You will walk in new authority now."

I have.

My hope had been for release from fear, but God gave me more than I expected. He used fear to draw me into a dependent relationship with him. He helped me realize that I had set up a self-protective wall nobody could penetrate. He helped me accept his love and reflect it to Shailesh and others. Now I've found my true purpose.

Shailesh and I now head up the Theophostic Prayer Ministry — the same ministry that helped me face my own spiritual obstacles and fears — at Two Rivers Church in Gilbert, Arizona.

I've gone from fear to peace, from confusion to clear thinking, from depression to joy, from despair to hope and from self-accusation to confidence in my heavenly father's love.

Now I trust him fully. He has given me a victorious life of freedom. I can fly in an airplane without any fear. I can grow long nails, instead of biting them until they bleed. Sexual thoughts and death scenarios no longer fill my mind. My health is better, and I can enjoy other centered relationships. I have control over my sugar cravings, since my desire to honor God is so great that it overcomes excessive eating of sweets.

fear failed

When my mind tries to follow its old path, the part of God that lives inside me reminds me of God's truth. Since I was familiar with the Bible, God has been able to bring helpful verses to my mind. God has wrapped me in praise and taken away the spirit of heaviness.

I no longer fear loss of control, for I have handed over control to God. He does a much better job than I can. I no longer fear separation, for my heavenly father has promised he will never leave me.

When my husband is late, I thank God for loving him and caring for him. I don't cower in a corner, crying. Shailesh and I have a happy marriage and a baby. I no longer fear his death or mine for I know the truth. When we die to self, we find everlasting life in Jesus Christ, our Savior and Lord. When we have Christ, fear fails.

facing my demons
the story of amir rana
written by jennifer wade

I was staring down the long, dark hallway of my Aunt Deepa's house. My cousin, Aisha's, room was the very last one. I felt as if I was being forced to walk the plank in some old pirate movie. With every step, my heart beat louder and louder. With every beat, I began to question what I would find, until I reached the slightly cracked door of my cousin's dimly lit room.

What is that awful noise? Something is wrong!

I took a deep breath and pushed through the door. In an instant, Aisha's eyes were upon me. I shook a little bit. There was no life in those eyes. They looked cold.

Is that her? I thought.

"Aisha?"

"Why have you come here?" she bellowed. I knew it was a god that had come upon her, because it was not her voice. It was a deep, horrifying, bone-chilling voice, unlike one I had ever heard before. It made the hairs on the back of my neck stand up straight, and suddenly, I shivered.

"Your … your … mother called us," I stuttered. "She said that we should come help you. What is going on? Are you all right?" I thought maybe the god could be reasoned with, but I soon realized that assumption was wrong.

"Help? Help! You cannot save her! She belongs to me now!" she roared in this horrible groaning sound. Her body began to spin all over the room as if Aisha was wres-

not by chance

tling with the god itself. Then she began to repeatedly throw her body against a wall. I felt scared, very scared, and extremely confused.

What in the world is going on here? Why did my aunt call us here?

I had no idea what to do. I began breathing and stood there, staring in shock.

Think rationally. Everything can be rationalized.

So I surveyed the room in a desperate search for some clue that might help explain this unimaginable situation.

My father, brother, aunt and uncle were huddled together in the left corner of the room. I assumed that they were trying to devise a plan to restrain Aisha. She was six months pregnant, and everyone was concerned about the baby. I joined them when they were ready, and we all pounced and pulled her down on the floor. We were all careful of the child that was growing inside her, and the god sensed this. It felt our love for Aisha and the child, so it roared with anger and jealousy.

Once we had Aisha on the floor, she was able to get hold of all four of us simultaneously and push us off of her all at the same time. It seemed as if she had the strength of three large men. This god had claimed the body of my cousin and was not going to give it up without a fight.

We picked ourselves up off the floor and hurried out of the room. I wanted to get as far away from the situation as I could, so I left the house and sat down outside so I could think clearly. I closed my eyes and sighed heavily. How did this happen? What was I going to do?

facing my demons

My mind was spinning out of control with questions. I was desperate for answers, and I had none. I thought maybe if I reviewed exactly what had happened the day before, I might see something that I missed. *Apply some logical thinking, Amir.* So I thought back to yesterday.

***

It was 2 on a Sunday afternoon when I started questioning everything I thought I knew. Like the shot at the beginning of a race, the telephone rang, and I was off and running.

Ring. Ring. Ring.

"Hello?" my father answered. "What's wrong? What's the matter? Is she all right?" There was a pause because the other person we could not hear was speaking to him.

"I'm not sure what you mean," my father continued. "A god has come upon Aisha?" I figured that the person on the other line was my aunt because Aisha is my cousin. "Of course. We will leave right away." My father turned to me and explained the grave situation.

"Amir, that was your Aunt Deepa. We have a problem here …" his voice trailed off. "There is a situation with your cousin, Aisha. They need all of us to go over there quickly. A god has come upon Aisha. It started yesterday, and they thought they could handle it, but it has gotten worse. The god is threatening to throw Aisha's body off the bed and kill the child growing inside of her. Go quickly and get your brother so we can drive to her house

not by chance

and help them!"

I found my brother and briefed him on the situation as we packed a bag and headed toward the car. My Aunt Deepa's house was about 20 minutes away. While we were driving, I started to wonder about what I would see when I got there. Having a degree in physics, I tried to develop some sort of rational explanation for what might be happening. I was beginning to get very curious.

Aisha has gone crazy, and my aunt just thinks she has been taken over. Yes, that would make more sense, I said to myself. I convinced myself that was what had happened, and by the time we arrived, I felt a lot better about it.

When Aunt Deepa saw us walking towards the house, she came running outside. *She must have been watching from the doorway,* I thought. My father and brother went inside with her to tend to Aisha. As I looked at the house, I felt a chill run up my spine. I started to get nervous as I climbed up the muddy steps, mostly because I heard screaming coming from inside. I couldn't make out the voice, and it certainly didn't sound like anyone I knew. I walked through the front door and started following the sound of the screaming. The screaming was then accompanied by loud banging. That's when it happened. That's when I saw what I will never forget: my cousin possessed by the fiercest demon I could have ever imagined. A god had overtaken her body, and all I had was my skepticism and some logic.

facing my demons

***

When I opened my eyes, I realized that I was getting nowhere.

This isn't helping, I thought, as I slowly peeled my back from the wall I was leaning on. I decided to abandon my logical thinking plan and go back inside to see if the others had come up with any ideas.

They are probably wondering about me.

I walked inside and looked at my family. They just stared back at me. No one knew what to say. Everyone was still visibly shaken. My aunt had barricaded the entrance to the room where Aisha was and tried to settle us by saying, "Things will calm down. The god comes and goes. Well … at least yesterday it did. I'll show you where you can sleep, and we will try to think of how to fix this tomorrow." She realized that everyone was looking for an answer that no one had. She sighed heavily, and we followed her to the opposite end of the house. I didn't think I would be able to sleep much knowing what had just happened, but I went through the motions anyway.

As the night pressed on, things in the house seemed calm. I couldn't hear any noise, and I wondered if the god had temporarily gone elsewhere. Maybe Aisha was sleeping? I wasn't sure how that worked. I couldn't stop my mind from racing with questions. So I lit a candle and scanned the room to see what my father and brother were up to. They were both asleep.

In a moment of desperation, I pulled a Nepali Bible

not by chance

out of my pack. A man had coincidentally dropped it by our house a few days earlier. I had scooped it up, thinking that it might come in handy. I looked at the cover intently. It was not the first time I had seen the Bible. In fact, I knew a little bit about it already. I leaned against the wall and closed my eyes.

"Think back to Evergreen," I whispered, "think back to college." And my mind fell backward over the previous four years.

***

I came to Evergreen College by chance. As a high school student in Nepal, I had initially intended on going to college in India. But in the end, my grades simply didn't measure up, and my parents weren't willing to chance a financial disaster on the hope that I would excel there. I was determined to find some way to go to college, and I got a hold of "Peterson's Complete Guide to Colleges" — a comprehensive guide to every 2- and 4-year college in the United States and Canada.

I actually took my first trip to the United States with my family in 1981. My father worked there for four years, and since I was already 7 years old, I went to school there for four years, also. I possessed excellent English skills because of the time I spent there, and I thought I would feel somewhat comfortable there. So, I applied to several colleges and studied hard for the SAT test.

I memorized hundreds of study questions and per-

facing my demons

formed very well on the practice SAT test. But when it came time to take the real test, I made a horrible mistake. I flipped an extra page in the test booklet and didn't realize it until after the test. Several of the answers that I filled in on the answer sheet were for the wrong questions. I still didn't do horribly — I scored 1,150 — but international students are held to a higher standard, and once again, my score didn't measure up.

The rejections from colleges started pouring in, and I was starting to lose all hope of continuing my education. One day, I received a letter from a small college in Spokane, Washington, called Evergreen College. They said that they had lost my application and would like for me to reapply so that they could take another look at it. I reapplied and they actually accepted me! I had no idea at this time that Evergreen was a Christian college. And since they gave me a very generous financial aid package, I felt it was an opportunity that I could not turn down. Off I went to Spokane, Washington.

My first year at Evergreen was horrible. I hated it there. I felt as if I had a sign on my head that read, "Not a Christian. Please convert." I was approached by several people daily about the power of the love of Jesus Christ. Most of the students there saw me as a golden opportunity to practice "saving" someone. I started to feel very angry, and I felt that the college had misrepresented itself. In fact, I marched into the admissions representative's office and let her know that I felt I had been duped. Nowhere on the application did it say that Evergreen was a Christian col-

not by chance

lege. Since I wasn't a Christian, and had no intention of becoming one, I felt that I didn't really belong there.

As time went on, I started to realize that Evergreen was a good school, and the financial aid was a huge incentive to stay there and try to finish. So, I made the best of an awkward situation by making friends with a few international students and some kids that were children of missionaries and had lived abroad for some time. They were the only people who seemed to understand me, and they didn't waste their time trying to change my views about religion. I didn't even have to study the Bible until it was almost time for graduation.

In my third year at the school, I opened the confirmed class schedule that the school had sent to my apartment and saw that they were requiring me to take a class on the Gospel of Matthew. "Oh, I won't take a Bible class," I said to myself out loud. "They can't make me take a Bible class!" With that, I marched down to my advisor's office and knocked on the door.

Dr. Smith will help me, I thought, as he beckoned me to come inside.

"Amir! Come in, come in! What's new?" he asked. Dr. Smith was someone I had come to admire.

"Dr. Smith, please, please, please get me out of this Bible class. I don't want to take a Bible class. I'm not a Christian," I pleaded.

"Look, Amir, I'm a Christian, but I lived in Asia for 20 years of my life. I have always been fascinated by their Buddhist religion. So every time I had an opportunity to

facing my demons

learn about it or experience something that had to do with it, I took it. And I learned so much about it, Amir! Look, you're in the same situation here. You're surrounded by Christians in a Christian environment. Why don't you just take the class and learn? It's not going to hurt you."

I thought about what he said for a few seconds. He was right. It was an opportunity to learn about something that I would never otherwise be able to learn about.

"Okay, Dr. Smith, I'll do it for you," I said, as if I was doing him some sort of favor by taking the class. So I took the Gospel of Matthew, and I hated every minute of it. I actually earned an A minus in a class that the teacher told me few people get an A minus in.

Yes, I got an A minus in the Gospel of Matthew. Matthew ... Matthew ... Matthew ...

***

"I have an idea!" I uttered out loud, as I snapped out of my reverie. In my Matthew class, I read a story about Jesus casting out demons from two men. I wondered if something from that story could be applied to this situation. I glanced over at my father and brother to make sure they were still asleep before I dared to pull out the Bible the neighbor had given me earlier. Since they had not stirred, I opened my pack and pulled out the book. I found the verse quite quickly under Matthew 8:28.

It read: "And when he was come to the other side into the country of the Gergesenes, there were two men pos-

not by chance

sessed with devils, coming out of the tombs, exceeding fierce, so that no man might pass by that way. And behold, they cried out, saying, 'What have we to do with thee, Jesus, thou Son of God? Art thou come hither to torment us before the time?' And there was a good way off from them a herd of many swine feeding. So the devils besought him, saying, 'If thou cast us out, suffer us to go away into the herd of swine.' And he said unto them, 'Go.' And when they were come out, they went into the herd of swine and behold, the whole herd of swine ran violently down a steep place into the sea, and perished in the waters."

I closed the book and returned it to its hiding place. With the story fresh in my mind, I got up and headed toward Aisha's room.

"This will work," I whispered, as I tried to convince myself.

When I arrived at the door, I stood quietly and listened.

Quiet.

As I crept inside, I could see the faint outline of her body in the bed.

Please be asleep, I thought to myself, as I came closer to where she lay. I decided against talking out loud since I was really scared. *No, it's better just to think the words,* I told myself. So I began.

I know that Jesus threw the spirits like these into the water. I want the same thing to happen right now. I want whatever this is to leave my cousin RIGHT NOW!

I opened my eyes as I asserted the last words, and Ai-

facing my demons

sha's legs began to shake violently. Her eyelids flipped open like a puppet, and she stood up in the bed.

"YOU!" the demon roared. "You are one of the people I want to kill!"

With that, she began to curse me and continued to threaten my life. I ran out of the room with the words "I want to kill you!" resounding in my head. I was dumbfounded. How could something hear my innermost thoughts? I did not speak out loud! Was there power behind this Jesus' name that even demons could sense? I was considerably shaken. I just didn't know what to believe anymore. I went back to the room but hardly slept at all. The next day, fearing for my life, I left.

When my father and brother returned home that evening, they told me that they decided to take Aisha to a Hindu priest who specialized in this sort of thing. Apparently, the priest channeled some sort of spirit, also, and his spirit tried to persuade my cousin's spirit to leave her body. He told the spirit that he had made the wrong choice and that my cousin was to be a mother. The demon demanded a specific sacrifice for the next day. It was done exactly as was requested, and it violently and reluctantly agreed to leave the body of my dear cousin with a smirk that gave my brother the chills.

It was then that I started questioning my beliefs, or better, lack of beliefs. I had read a little and heard a lot about Jesus Christ during my time at Evergreen, but I wasn't convinced that this Jesus was someone I wanted to be connected with. But I was sure he had some kind of

not by chance

power. How could a man with no religious faith utter the name of Jesus in his head and see a demon respond so violently? I didn't even believe in Jesus, but I know what I saw. How could that have happened if this Jesus was a falsity?

Though I went over and over the scene again in my head, trying to figure out some rational reason that the demon had responded to my thoughts, I couldn't find any. So I decided to head back to the United States. I wanted to explore this new curiosity I had about Jesus. I also wanted to continue pursuing a relationship with Elizabeth.

Elizabeth was a fellow Evergreen graduate who I had bonded closely with in school. Around the time we graduated, we realized that we had fallen in love. We did not think it could last because of our differences, but we ended up staying in touch and "dating" long distance, while she spent a few years in Korea after college. After the incident with Aisha, we decided to meet up in Hawaii, and I left Nepal with great anticipation. After our meeting, Elizabeth decided she wanted to give our relationship a try, so she moved to Chicago, Illinois, where I was going to be working.

Once I was settled in the United States, I began to think about Jesus often. I took out the Bible that the man had given me in Nepal and started to read it.

This Jesus is not a bad guy, I thought. *His ideas and thoughts, they seem pretty good.* I started to think that I had previously misjudged the Bible and Jesus because of the way I was approached at Evergreen. I decided that this

facing my demons

Jesus knew what he was talking about, and he was a decent guy. *Not a bad way to raise a family*, I noted.

With that in mind, I attended a few different churches with a few different people. I never really felt comfortable at any of them, but I tried to learn as much about Jesus as I could.

During that time, Elizabeth and I were getting more serious. Things were good for a while, and I even gave her a key to my apartment and access to my credit card. We did everything together. But for some reason or other, things always went astray. The differences between us loomed large in our relationship, and neither of us was sure we had the strength to overcome those differences. After four years of dating, we split up. We were both devastated. Elizabeth continued teaching. I went off to graduate school.

A few months passed, and she decided to stop by my apartment when I was not there. I guess she still had the key I had given her. I had spent the last three months missing her tremendously and fighting a deep depression. Just when I was getting back on track, she came by to borrow a Tupperware container. When I came home, I saw that she had written me a note.

Amir, I borrowed a Tupperware container. Hope you don't mind. I will bring it back to you ASAP. Thanks a lot, Elizabeth.

The note brought to me a flood of emotion and reminded me of how much I missed her. I missed our friendship, and I missed confiding in her. I was a mess. I

not by chance

didn't understand why she kept coming back into my life again and again. I decided that I needed answers, some sort of direction. I thought about how I had been spending all this time learning about the Bible but not really connecting with Jesus in my heart. I knew, at that moment, that I wanted to pray sincerely, so I went to my bedroom, shut the door and expectantly asked, "God, why has Elizabeth returned to my life again?"

That is when it happened. An audible, strong voice promptly answered me. "Amir, I am getting her ready to be your wife. I have plans for your life together."

Tingles crept down my spine. I glanced around, but no one was there. I'd never heard a voice so clearly or so plainly before. I'd never heard a voice that I knew with all my heart was God. And yet, this voice *was* God. I just knew. God had a plan for me, and it was with Elizabeth.

Knowing that God had spoken to me, I couldn't deny him any longer. I decided to call up my friend, Chris. Chris was a college friend that I trusted. On the phone, I told him of my experience with God speaking to me. He insisted that we meet so that we could talk face to face. So we met for lunch at an Indian restaurant. Just as we finished ordering our food and the waitress disappeared from sight, he pulled a napkin from the holder and started drawing. It was a diagram of me on one side and God on the other.

"Amir, there is a separation between God and man. The result of sin is death. The way to life is through God. You can never get to God on your own. You need a

facing my demons

bridge, and the bridge is Jesus Christ." I looked at him and nodded. He continued to ask questions.

"If you die today, will you go to heaven?"

I was not sure about that one.

He continued, "After the bridge is complete, where will you be? Are you the man running away from the cross? Are you the man standing by the door waiting to come in? Or are you the man rejoicing in the presence of God?"

"Chris, I am the guy that rings the doorbell and runs the other way," I answered.

"Fair enough. I will pray for you," he responded.

After the semester ended, I decided to go back to Nepal. I still couldn't stop thinking about the voice that I had heard and the bridge picture that Chris had shown me at the restaurant. As I traveled, I felt a wonderful, loving spirit around me. I felt happy, safe and content. I had been back for about a week, and I was lying in bed one night when I felt something. It felt like a weight being lifted from my body. It felt *wonderful.* God asked me to come to him that night and I did. I said, "God, I give myself to Jesus Christ, whatever that means." I felt so right and complete that I rolled over and fell into a peaceful sleep.

The next day, I went to see a Christian pastor in Nepal. I told him what had happened and he said, "My friend, you have just become a Christian. Congratulations. You know what the cost is. This is not a friendly country for Christianity. Your parents are Hindus. That is the cost."

I spoke with him for a while and really thought about

not by chance

what he had said. Something inside me said that I would be able to meet those costs he spoke of and that I had made the right decision.

When I returned to the United States for school, I felt stronger than I had ever felt in my whole life. I saw Elizabeth, and I told her that I was over her completely. It was not the truth, but I wanted to see how God would work things out for us. She says that she noticed a distinct change in my demeanor and that I was "glowing." We began dating again, and in a few months, we were married. We had loved each other for so long, but now it was with a new depth and strength. Now that I had a personal relationship with Christ, I felt confident that I could handle anything that came my way.

In so many ways, that decision changed my life. I was stronger, more confident, at peace and content. I knew that God had a plan for my life, and that took the pressure off me to forge a way by myself. He made things happen that I never could, no matter how hard I tried. He brought Elizabeth back to me. He brought me my wife.

Elizabeth and I began attending Lake City Church together. It was there that, through the grace of God, I was able to take the next step on my journey. It was a step into spiritual freedom. We had a guest speaker, Sam, who was a convert from Hinduism to Christianity. I thought at the time that it was a strange coincidence. During his sermon, he expressed that he felt the need to pray for me specifically. I wondered why, but I did as he asked and met Sam and Pastor Tom in an office after the service.

facing my demons

I remember peeking through the door and seeing the two men inside. They both shook my hand and invited me to pray with them. We all knelt down on the floor together, and Pastor Sam looked directly at me as he spoke.

Immediately, my mind was struggling with an intense internal battle. As Pastor Sam began to name specific prayer concerns, my eyes seemed to twist and turn beneath my lids, forming knots that caused tension near my brain. But when he named the presence of demons, I could hear Elizabeth's gasps from across the room as she reacted to the same strange phenomenon I felt. My face contorted into unnatural knots, and my body began to shake. I placed my hand below me, trying to steady myself, but the shaking continued, steadily, as if I were sitting on a dryer or driving on a bumpy road. I couldn't shake it. I couldn't stop it.

Pastor Sam paused. "I want you to confess Jesus Christ as your Lord and Savior and say that you are now the seed of Abraham," he instructed.

As I opened my mouth to speak the words, I found that I had to struggle to get out, "Jesus Christ is my Lord and Savior …" and I physically could not say the rest.

By this time, my entire body and face were shaking. My tongue seemed to pull out from my mouth and under my chin, as if I were choking. Not only could I not utter the words, "I am the seed of Abraham," I couldn't utter any words at all.

I could feel the red-hot heat creeping up my neck and my eyes bulging from their sockets. Again, I tried to force

not by chance

out the words, but all I could manage was a soft hum. Soon, I remembered why.

When I was 13 years old, I was dedicated to the powerful Hindu god, Shiva. It seemed Shiva did not want to give me up without a fight.

Sam prayed, "Shiva, you are to release the claim that you have on this child of God, Amir. Jesus wants Amir as his, and he commands that you release him."

Sam prayed specifically against Shiva for 45 minutes until I was finally able to spit out the words, "I am the seed of Abraham." And after 45 painful minutes, that demon, like the one Jesus cast out from my cousin, left my body.

Jesus triumphed over all things.

Today, I am finally able to say with a happy heart and soul that I belong completely to Jesus Christ. Elizabeth and I now attend Two Rivers Church, a church we helped Pastor Tom start after our prayer time together.

I've gone from angry to peaceful, sad to joyful, depressed to happy and hopeless to hopeful. It's a transformation that only a Savior I never believed in could have made in the life of a logical skeptic like me.

Jesus Christ is my Lord. I am the seed of Abraham.

there with me
the story of cynthia
written by amanda lawrence

I picked up the remote control off the living room floor and placed it in the remote holder, as I straightened the magazines on the floor next to the recliner and folded today's newspaper, placing it in the recycle bin next to the door leading into the kitchen. As I was heading down the hall to the boys' rooms with the folded laundry, the doorbell rang. I placed the laundry basket on the hall floor and walked to the front door, opening it to find two policemen on my doorstep. I took a quick inventory of where my family was: George at work, Samuel at the library, Tom at his friend's house and Connor next door.

I wonder why they're here. Did something happen to one of the kids? To George? It's never good to find police on my doorstep, although I should be used to the sight, I thought.

"Good afternoon, ma'am," the shorter, blonde-haired officer greeted me.

"Afternoon," I replied, my heart in my throat and my pulse pounding.

"Do you know where your son is?" he questioned me.

"I have three sons. Which one are you referring to?" I asked.

"Tom, your middle one," he responded.

"He's at a friend's house. Why? What happened?"

"We witnessed him selling drugs to some neighbor-

not by chance

hood kids. We'd like to search his room," the other, dark-headed officer replied.

"Come in. Let me call my husband. Can you wait a minute?"

"Yes," the first officer answered, both of them entering the foyer and standing just inside the door.

I walked into the kitchen to call my husband at work.

"George, some policemen are here to search Tom's room. They think he was selling drugs at the park."

"You need to go to my room and get rid of my stash," he responded.

"What? Are you kidding me?" I reacted, not believing that he was more concerned with the police finding his drugs than about Tom. "I've got to go. The police are waiting in the living room. I just wanted to let you know what was going on." I hung up without waiting for a response.

"Tom's room is this way," I directed, walking down the hall to the second door on the right. "Go ahead and look around." I left them alone and went back to the living room, dropping to the couch. The phone rang, and I rushed into the kitchen.

"Hello?"

"Are they still there? Are they searching the entire house? They can't find my stuff," my husband rattled off to me.

"Why don't you come home if you're so concerned with them finding something?" I answered.

"I'm not coming home. You take care of it." He hung up.

there with me

I sighed, dropped the phone back in its cradle and walked back into the living room.

The policemen were just returning to the same place. "We didn't find anything, ma'am," the blonde declared.

"When Tom comes home, I'll question him about it. If he did in fact sell drugs, then I'll make sure he's held accountable," I replied.

"We won't search anymore of the house. Thank you for your assistance," the dark-headed officer proclaimed, resting his hands on his hips, right above his gun.

"You're welcome." The words were barely out of my mouth when the phone rang again.

"We'll let you get that. Thanks again," the blonde expressed, following his partner out the front door.

"Hello?" I breathed once I reached the receiver.

"Are they still there?"

"No, they just left. They didn't find anything in Tom's bedroom."

"What about mine? Did they search anywhere else?"

"No, just Tom's room."

"I'll be home soon," and then he hung up.

I paced around the living room. Waiting has never been a strong suit of mine, and I didn't know what to do with my time. I walked into the kitchen, wondering if I should start dinner. I looked at the clock and decided it was still too early to start cooking. The dishes were done, kitchen clean, nothing I could really do to bide my time. I turned around and walked back into the living room. *I've already picked up this room. Nothing here to do but pace,*

not by chance

I thought. I spotted the forgotten basket of laundry. Leaning down to pick it up, I walked down the hall to Tom's room first. Looking around, it didn't look as though the police had only searched it 10 minutes ago. Tom's pajamas lay in a heap next to his bed, which at least he made that morning before school. Baseball cards were strewn across his desk and a pile of books rested on the corner. I walked over to his dresser, opening the top drawer to put his socks away. It was a little disorganized, but it looked like Tom had been searching for a pair of socks, not like the police had been searching for a bag of drugs.

I left his room and put the rest of the laundry away in the other boys' rooms.

20 minutes later, George walked in the door.

"Is Tom home yet?" he asked nervously.

"Not yet. I want you to get me your stash," I replied.

He ambled down the hall to his room and returned a few minutes later with a handful of little bags. I took them from him and walked into the bathroom, shutting the door behind me. After emptying the bags into the toilet, I flushed.

George pounded on the door. "What do you think you're doing?" he raged.

I washed my hands, taking my time. I was not willing to look at my angry husband quite yet. His lack of caring about what he had just put me through by not coming home to help me deal with the police and his selfishness over concerns about himself and not Tom frustrated me. He pounded on the door again. My heart throbbed in my

there with me

chest, and my palms began to sweat, knowing that George would be very angry about losing his precious pot.

I opened the door.

"Getting rid of your stash, like you asked. It's against your probation, and I told you not to have it in the house anymore." I squeezed around him and walked back down the hall into the living room. I heard him rampaging down the hall behind me. I turned, watching him storm into the room, his hands clenched into fists and his nostrils flared.

I hope he doesn't hit me, but it needed to be done. I had to flush what he had left. I'm only protecting my kids, I kept repeating in my mind.

"Why'd you go and do that? That's all I've got. And I was already missing an ounce," he fumed. "The police have already come and gone, and they didn't find it."

I turned to look at him. "When did you realize you were missing some? And the police may be back. I told them I'd talk to Tom."

"I noticed it missing last night."

"Why didn't you tell me you had some missing? Didn't you think that one of the boys may have taken it?"

"I thought about telling you, but figured, why should I? You do your own thing, I do mine. You don't tell me everything," he announced.

I just glared at him, speechless.

Tom walked in from the kitchen, having come in the back door.

"Hi."

"Tom, where have you been?" I asked.

not by chance

"At Jerry's house."

"The police were just here, searching for drugs in your room. They said they saw you selling some at the park. Were you?" I demanded.

He glanced to George and then to me. "Yeah, but I can explain."

"Explain it to the police," I demanded, going to the phone and calling them back. When the police arrived, Tom was nervous and scared.

"He admitted he was selling drugs. Talk to him," I murmured, admitting them into the house.

Tom confessed as soon as he saw the policemen. "I did give some drugs to a group of guys, but only because they threatened me. They said they would hit me with a bar if I didn't bring them some drugs," he cried.

"We know who they are and know that they're bad kids. We won't press charges, but never give them anything again. Do you have any more drugs?" the dark-headed policeman asked.

"No. I gave them all I had," Tom explained.

"Are there any other drugs in the house?" he asked George and me.

"No," George defended with a frown on his face.

The police soon left, and I sent Tom to his room. George almost seemed proud of Tom's actions, not concerned at all that his son had almost been charged with possession or intent to sell.

"Why are we living this life for our children?" I asked him.

there with me

He just grinned.

I grew up in San Jose, California, with my sister, who was seven years older than me. She was my world. She raised me because my alcoholic parents weren't home much, so she was my surrogate mother, my teacher, my friend, my everything. When my parents were home, if they weren't passed out, they fought. They used household items to hurt each other, like a crystal platter with sharp edges my mother used to slice my father's cheeks. Our house was decorated with broken doors and lots of bruises.

One night, I heard my parents amble in the house, drunk and reeking of cheap beer. My mother told my father that he had better move the gun from his side table or she was going to shoot him. I heard his footsteps tromp unsteadily down the main hallway, a pause, and then a pop that pierced my ears and sent me sprinting to my sister's room. The next day, we found out that Mom had shot the wall behind her and not my father. I looked at that bullet hole for several years as a reminder of that night.

I found comfort in sleeping in my sister's room. She moved into her own apartment when she was 18, and shortly after, my parents divorced. I lived with my mom, and my dad started to see his high school sweetheart.

"I know they had an affair while we were still married," my mom would complain between swigs of liquor.

My mom and I lived in a trailer in San Jose after my parents divorced. She married her neighbor, who was an alcoholic, which caused friction between her and me.

not by chance

About a year after their marriage, my mom woke up and realized that their relationship just wasn't right. We moved to San Diego, and she dated and we moved in with another guy for about six months. Then one day, she went bowling and met Greg, the man who would become my stepfather. He treated her as she deserved, opening doors for her and responding to her with respect and love.

When I was 12, my sister moved to Sacramento, and I looked forward to visiting her. I missed her headstrong, stand-her-ground attitude towards life. I was also at the curious stage in life about my body and sex, and I had questions I couldn't ask my mom. My sister pulled out *Joy of Sex* and shared some of the details of the book. The book must have triggered something in her live-in boyfriend, Bud, because he cornered me one day while she was at work.

"So, you're interested in what sex is all about, huh?" he asked.

"I'm just curious," I stuttered, nervous at how close he was getting.

"I can show you better than some book," he drawled, grabbing me and kissing me. I tried pushing him away, but he was stronger than me. He pulled the bottom of my t-shirt from its place tucked in my shorts and moved his hand up my still developing chest. I cringed away from him, but his hand followed, and he grabbed me around my neck and pulled me into him. He moved his kisses from my mouth down my neck. "Isn't this better than some pictures in some book?" he asked.

there with me

"No! Stop!" I cried. He ignored me and pulled me into the bedroom. I was frightened to death of what he was doing to me, and pain ripped through my body. I lay shuddering on the bed after he was done. He got dressed and threw my t-shirt and shorts at me.

"Get dressed. And you're not going to tell anyone. The last thing you want to do is hurt your sister, and telling her would devastate her. Not only that, but she wouldn't believe you anyhow." He left the room, and I curled into a ball, crying.

Every time I visited, Bud would molest me. There was even one time, while my sister lay sleeping on the other side of me, that he fondled me. I couldn't get away from his touch. Finally, when I was 16, I stood up to him.

"You ever touch me again, and I'm gonna hurt you," I threatened. A couple of years later, he and my sister, now his wife, moved to Germany, where he was transferred.

The next time I saw them, I was 22 and living in Arkansas. They had moved back to Texas, so I drove down to visit them. While I was there, I witnessed the evidence of why my once headstrong sister was now a wimp. She and Bud had been fighting when he grabbed her around the neck and threw her up against the wall, strangling her. She whimpered and begged him to stop, telling him she was sorry. He stopped.

When she had gone to work, Bud attacked me, wanting to pick up where he left off when I was 16. I had to fight him off. I left, driving back to Arkansas without saying goodbye to my sister. I really haven't talked to her

not by chance

since, though I've tried to. She stopped talking to everyone — me, my mom and the rest of the family.

When I was 13, I met a friend named Cathy who accepted me as I was, overweight and insecure. I never fit in, and I wanted to be accepted.

"You'll like this. It will make you happy and euphoric," she said, handing me a rolled joint.

"What is it?" I asked, taking it.

"Pot. I like it," she responded.

I took a drag and started coughing. The sweet-sour smell of the smoking joint filled my nostrils. I took another drag, this time more slowly, and felt the smoke enter my chest and up through my nostrils. The colors in her bedroom were more vibrant, and the pleasant sensation of not caring about my life invaded me. My hands started to tremble, and my mouth felt dry, but I continued to inhale until the joint was gone. Lying back in her beanbag chair, I spread my arms wide and sighed. "Ah, I feel good."

"Told you so," Cathy replied, finished with her joint and lying sprawled on her bed.

After that, we tested crystal meth and acid, but I returned to marijuana as my preferred drug, my preferred natural depressant for the next 25 years. In high school, I fit in with the drug crowd. They didn't care about anything but drugs.

I don't even know how many boyfriends I went through from 13 to 18. There were too many to count. My sophomore year of high school, I dated a 28-year-old man who lived with his mom because she had custody of his 4-

… there with me

year-old son. I always searched for someone to help, and helping people always turned around to hurt me. He wasn't working, but I was, so I took care of him. He in turn stole from me. Then I dated a fireman in his 30s that my mom was attracted to. After having sex with me, he had sex with her. I didn't want to have anything to do with him, and my mom dated him for a while before realizing herself that he was a player. It wasn't until I was 19 that I met someone who I thought was good enough.

I listened to the CB radio a lot and would go to a local donut shop where a lot of truckers hung out. One day, I met George. He was married with two kids, but I still asked him if I could ride in his truck, something that I had always wanted to do. We went down to the San Diego beach. I was promiscuous and a drug addict at the time, and we enjoyed sex near the beach.

"Why are all the good guys taken?" I asked after our time together.

He just kissed me in response. The next day, he called. "Hey, babe. How you doing?" he asked.

"I'm good. How about yourself? Where are you at?" I replied.

"I'm really good. Still remembering yesterday and what fun we had. I just left Sacramento."

"Where are you headed now?" I asked.

"Back to San Diego. I've got to see you again. I'm leaving my wife and want you to come on the road with me," he answered.

"You're leaving your family? For me?" I asked, flabber-

not by chance

gasted.

"What can I say? You're what I want," he rejoined.

"I'll go with you. Absolutely," I declared, happy to get away from my mom and San Diego. "This is exciting. I've always wanted to travel, and now I get to go with you."

For the next two years, we traveled cross-country. I settled in Arkansas while he drove his rig, and two years later, I found out I was pregnant.

I held the pregnancy test in my limp right hand and dropped down onto the closed toilet lid. *A baby. I'm going to have a baby. What am I going to do?* I thought, stunned. What I thought was the flu had turned out to be morning sickness.

How am I going to tell George? He said he never wanted any more kids, and he might think a baby will tie him down. Will he think that I got pregnant on purpose? I'll have to tell him next time he calls. So many thoughts were whizzing around my head.

"George, I'm pregnant," I told him one day when he called from the road.

"Whose is it? It's not mine," he replied.

"Yes, it is. I haven't been with anyone else since we got together," I revealed, hurt that he would believe I would cheat on him while he was away.

"Let me call you back. I'm going to talk to my dad," he stated, then hung up.

An hour later, he called back. "Well, I guess we have to get married," were the first words out of his mouth.

"Yeah, I guess so," I agreed.

there with me

The next time he was in town, we drove down to the courthouse to get married before a justice of the peace. We arrived at lunchtime, and there was only one person there. Our short ceremony was interrupted numerous times by the ringing phones and people walking between us as they returned to work. Not the way I imagined my wedding day growing up, that was for certain.

When my son was 10 months old, I found out that George had cheated on me. Big surprise. I called my mom, and she came to pick Samuel and me up in Arkansas to take me home to San Diego. Not long after returning, I found out I was pregnant again.

"Mom, I'm pregnant again," I told her, holding 11-month-old Samuel in my arms.

"What do you plan on doing? You don't have a job. Are you planning on reconciling with George?" she asked.

"No, there's no chance for reconciliation between us. I still don't know what I'm going to do. I still have time to decide."

"Don't wait too long. Have you thought about adoption? I know you have always wanted to be a mother, but I just don't see how you can raise two kids on your own, especially since you're living with me now and not working at all," she replied.

"I don't think I could carry a child for nine months and then just give it up for adoption. That would be too hard," I whispered. "I better put Samuel down for his nap." I left the kitchen and went to the guest room that Samuel and I were living in.

not by chance

A week before my opportunity to terminate the pregnancy passed, I went to the local clinic. I dressed in a light green sundress with strappy sandals in an attempt to feel like a lady. The last time I really remember wearing a dress was on my wedding day. When I got to the clinic, a nurse ushered me into a white room with only a few magazine racks for decoration. After waiting for 45 minutes, perusing the year-old magazines, a doctor in a white lab coat entered the room.

"Good afternoon," he greeted me, putting his glasses on as he sat down at the small table against the wall, opening my chart. "I understand you're here to terminate your pregnancy?"

"Yes," I answered, shifting in my chair.

He looked through my chart a little more and did a five-minute rundown on the process I would go through. After finishing, he closed the chart and got up. "Okay, if you'll put on this paper gown and lie on the table, I'll be back in a few minutes with the nurse, and we'll get started." He left the room, not asking me if I had any questions or concerns.

I dressed in the flimsy paper gown and lay down on the hard examination table. I folded my arms across my chest and stared up at the fluorescent lights, trying to numb myself to the events that I would soon endure. The doctor and nurse came back into the room and proceeded to get ready for the abortion. I put my feet in the stirrups, and then the anesthesia they gave me took effect and all went black. They told me afterward that it was a girl. I

there with me

killed my little girl.

I lay in bed for two weeks, feeling like a failure and a horrible person. I was drug free at the time, believing that I was mentally stable and able to handle what I had done. But I was devastated. I felt that I couldn't carry a child to full term just to give her up, but now I wish I had done just that.

I finally crawled out of bed and started to search for a job. My best girlfriend, Janet, told me about a position at her company, so I applied and got the job. She introduced me to a fellow co-worker.

"Cindy, I want you to meet George. He rents a room from me as well, so you may see him when you come over," Janet mentioned.

"Nice to meet you, but I hate your name," I replied.

He looked at me quizzically. "Uh, nice to meet you, too. Sorry you hate my name," he replied, a little stunned.

"Please don't take offense. My ex-husband's name is George, and our divorce is still fresh," I told him.

"No offense taken," he commented.

That's where our friendship began. Once again, like my older boyfriend in high school, I found someone that I needed to take care of. He was an alcoholic and a drug addict, full of sob stories, and I just wanted to take care of him. When he was just 9 years old, his mother died in his arms of breast cancer. His father worked as an architect, so he had pretty much anything he wanted growing up. Our first date was to a drive-in movie. Soon we moved in together. One thing we had in common was our drug addic-

not by chance

tion. We smoked pot together, and he would also drink. However, I never drank because of my parents' alcoholism while I was growing up.

A few years after we moved in together, George wanted to spice up our sex life by participating in a threesome. I didn't agree to it, but he brought home a woman anyhow. What's more, she was a friend of mine. They started to have sex in front of me, but I left, upset that he would put me in that position. When I got home hours later, he was alone and promising never to do that again. Needless to say, Julie and I ended our friendship after that, and I found myself struggling to fully trust my female friends, even those who'd offered nothing but love and trust.

Soon, George lost his job. I was working at a pharmacy now, enjoying my job, but it didn't pay enough to support both of our habits as well as place food on the table. I started to steal money and drugs from the pharmacy so we could pay the bills by selling drugs on the side. I picked up his mentality of doing whatever I needed to do to get what I wanted, even though I was raised with the belief that you lived on what you had and made do with it.

After five years of living together, I gave George the news.

"I'm pregnant."

He turned from the TV, his eyes glassy from the high he was on. "It's not mine. Whose kid is it?" he denied.

"It is yours," I replied, a feeling of déjà vu sweeping me. "I haven't been with anyone else since we got to-

there with me

gether."

He turned back to the TV and took a swig from his beer. "What do you want me to say? Congratulations?"

"I don't expect you to say anything. I wanted to let you know that you're going to be a father."

"Now I know."

I turned from him, wiping tears and expecting more of a response. I went to check on Samuel, already in bed because he had school the next day. Just like when I was pregnant the first time, I abstained from drugs. When I was eight months pregnant, tired and huge, George and I drove with a couple of friends to Las Vegas so we could get married.

"Dad is paying for this entire trip," George mentioned to our friends as he drove down the strip. We found a hotel and checked in. "I'm going to the bar," he told me, handing me my small suitcase.

"I'm going upstairs to rest. I'm tired," I told him.

"Fine. We'll go to the wedding chapel in a few hours." He turned away from me and made a beeline for the bar, weaving through dinging slot machines and card tables.

Hours later, still tired, I stood before a cheesy justice of the peace who pronounced me and my drunken fiancée husband and wife. A month and a day later, we welcomed another son, Tom, into the world.

I liked how I was feeling after the pregnancy, having given up drugs. I wanted George to stop as well, believing it was time to grow up. For another year and a half, I was drug free. Then George started to taunt me. "Oh, this is so

not by chance

good. Wouldn't you want some? Doesn't that smell good?" He waved his smoking joint underneath my nose. "Oh, that's right, you don't do this anymore." He took a drag.

I caved and started smoking again. Our house was a busy house with many people coming to get high or buy drugs. The harder I tried to do good and make it better, the worse it got. After another four years, I got pregnant with my third son. The drug activity in the house only got worse. I knew we needed to get out of our neighborhood and out of San Diego where drugs surrounded us. My dad had moved to Arizona, so I went onto the Internet to look for a job. I scheduled six interviews for a Friday afternoon. After three of them, I returned to my hotel room and listened to a message offering me a job. "We need you in three weeks," the Human Resources woman told me when I called back.

"I need to talk to my husband still, and I'll need at least a week to move here," I responded.

I called my husband after getting off the phone with the HR woman.

"I got a job," I told him as soon as he came to the phone. "I'll be making more money than my job in San Diego, too."

"Then I guess we'll be moving to Arizona," he remarked. It didn't matter much to him, as he was still jobless himself.

We soon moved to Gilbert, Arizona. Without a place to move into, we stayed in a motel room for one week. Trying to start a new job and having all five of us in one

there with me

motel room made for a stressful week. After two months, George found a job. Almost everyone he worked with did meth or smoked pot. He became withdrawn, coming home from work and holing himself up in his room. We lived this way for five years. The more withdrawn he became because of drugs, the angrier I became. I was a horrible parent, always screaming and yelling at my kids for no reason. I had no desire to provide my husband with my wifely duties, and one of the few things we had in common anymore was our fighting with each other.

I was at the end of my rope. I was ready to give up. I didn't have an identity of my own. I became dead to myself with no hopes or dreams. George sabotaged my life. When I joined a gym to lose weight, he cancelled my membership. When I tried to decorate our house, he didn't like anything I bought or any of my grandparents' pictures, and he even deliberately ruined them by removing them from their frames and folding them in half.

Samuel started attending youth group with a friend of his and would come home excited. I was raised to believe that church was for good people, and my family believed they weren't good enough for church, so I didn't have any knowledge of God. One Wednesday night, Samuel was ready to walk out the door to go to youth when I stopped him.

"You're not going anywhere tonight. You haven't cleaned your room or done the dishes," I told him.

"Can't I do it when I get back? Youth is tonight, and I don't want to miss it," he pleaded.

not by chance

"No, you know the deal, chores not done, you don't go anywhere," I replied.

"That's unfair! You know I'll do them when I get back. You just want to prevent me from going," he raged, storming at me and lining up toe to toe before me.

Surprised because he had always avoided altercations, I stood my ground.

"I'm your mother, and I'm telling you, you're not going anywhere tonight. Go to your room. Clean it. Then come back here and do the dishes," I spit at him.

"Get out of my face, or I'm calling the cops," he threatened, glaring at me.

"Be my guest," I told him, handing him the phone.

He dialed 911, but hung up before talking to the assistant on the other side. "Forget it!" He stormed from the house.

Shaken, I dropped into the chair at the kitchen table.

Where did that come from? I thought to myself. *That's so unlike him. If he's so passionate about going to church, I'd better check this out. I need to make sure that he's not part of a cult.*

Decided on what I would do, I got up from the table and started to remove the rest of the dinner dishes, putting them in the sink for Samuel to do once he came home.

The doorbell rang, and I went to answer it. The police stood on the other side. "We received a hang up call from this residence. We're checking on you. Is there a problem?" one asked.

"My son called but stormed out. I think I know where

there with me

he's gone. Please come in. I'll call him," I told them. They moved into the living room, and I went to the kitchen to call Samuel's friend, certain he would be at his house. I was correct. "You need to come home. The police have shown up because of your call, and you're going to explain to them why you called," I told him.

"I'm on my way," he responded. Less than five minutes later, he walked in the front door. The police stood up from their seats on the couch.

"This is Samuel. He called you," I told them, still sitting in the La-Z-Boy.

"Why'd you call?" the taller of the policemen asked.

"I threatened my mom that I would call the police, and she followed through with my threat. I wanted to go somewhere tonight, and she told me I couldn't cause I didn't finish my chores. I got mad," he told them, shuffling from side to side.

"Your mom was in perfect rights to tell you not to go anywhere. If we have to come back here, someone will be going to jail, and it won't be your mom," the same policeman replied.

"Yes, sir," Samuel whispered. The police left.

"I'm sorry, Mom. I was mad you weren't letting me go."

"You're forgiven. I'm coming to church with you on Sunday. I want to find out what it is about this place that has you so passionate," I answered.

"Cool! I'm glad you're coming. I know you'll like it," he declared, a grin on his face.

not by chance

"Get into the kitchen and wash the dishes. They're still waiting for you," I informed him.

The next Sunday, I attended church for the first time in my life. The moment I walked into Two Rivers, the people welcomed me and loved on me, treating me with respect even though they did not know me. As I walked through the sanctuary to find a seat, people continued to smile at me and greet me. I sat down and looked over the bulletin, glancing around to watch other people filter through the doors toward their own seats. Though there was a hum around the room as everyone chatted with each other, I felt that there was a serene presence in the room.

Worship service began. The worship leader started with a fast, upbeat song, and people around me clapped their hands. After another jubilant song, the music slowed and people around me raised their hands. I didn't understand the significance of them lifting their arms, even though the song talked about praising the name of God. I looked around to the people surrounding me, and I saw smiles and joy exuding from everyone. I had a tingly feeling running up and down throughout my body, and I started to cry. I continued to bawl throughout the rest of worship. Then Pastor Tom started to preach the sermon. I stared up at him in the pulpit. *He's talking about me. He doesn't even know me, and he's talking about me,* I thought. Amazed, I continued to listen to him talk about the myths that make our lives miserable.

When I got home from church that afternoon, I told George about it.

there with me

"You need to come with me next week. The worship service was like nothing I ever experienced. I cried through most of it. Then the pastor got up, and I felt like he was talking about me."

"That's great that you enjoyed yourself, but church isn't my kind of scene. Go back if you like, but don't expect me to go with you," he retorted.

"I plan on going back next Sunday," I replied.

"Fine." He turned his attention back to the football game on TV, and I moved into the kitchen to start lunch.

The next Sunday, I returned and experienced the same reception from the people, and the worship service affected me the same way. I continued to wipe my eyes as I tried to read the screen with the words and sing along.

This is where I'm supposed to be right now. I'm going to come back until I understand what it is about this place that has affected me so much, I thought, as I sat down and Pastor Tom started preaching his sermon. And I did return. For Bible studies and for Sunday school and church. I shared a little bit about my life and was amazed when the people in my Bible study still loved on me. Having been overweight my entire life, I was used to people judging me by my appearance. I was never allowed to show who I truly was while growing up, and these people didn't put me down for the life I had led, even though I was ashamed and afraid to show them who I really was.

After attending services for three months, at the end of June, I attended a prayer and praise function. It was my first experience at that function, and by the end of the

not by chance

night, Pastor Tom approached and asked me if I was ready to surrender my life fully to Jesus Christ. I told him I was. As he prayed over me, I felt electricity shooting through my body. My toes tingled and waves of prickles moved up my legs into my arms and down to my fingers, almost as though I had just stepped on a live, exposed wire or I had been struck by lightning.

"I surrender. Do with me what you will. My life is changed," I prayed. Immediately, my anger went away. An overwhelming sense of peace and joy filled my body, and I laughed. I didn't understand it, but I liked it.

I stopped yelling at my children, and they didn't understand why the little things they had done before that would cause me to explode in anger didn't get any response at all. George would try to fight with me by yelling, but I would just smile and ignore him, which only made him angrier. I started to attend Pastor Tom's First Things First series where I learned scriptures, what it was like to become a Christian and the kinds of things I would experience, God's character and a quick timeline of the Bible.

One Sunday, a couple of weeks after surrendering my life to Christ, I came home from church. George pulled his truck behind my car and removed my car's battery. He was drunk and angry at me for finding something else to occupy my time. Yelling and screaming, I didn't understand anything he was saying.

"Go to your room and sober up. We'll talk later," I told him.

there with me

He grabbed me and threw me down on the couch. Pouncing on top of me, he started to choke me and slap my face. I tried to toss my head from side to side to avoid his slaps, but his hands around my neck held me still. Samuel pulled him off me, and George turned and attacked him. "Get away from me, you brat. Think you're some big tough guy, well, I'm still your dad," he slurred, slapping him upside the head.

"You're not my father. You're drunk. Leave my mom alone!" he raged.

I crawled from the couch and dialed 911, the hardest thing I had ever done. The police arrived quickly, having heard the hitting and yelling in the background when I called.

"Do you want to press charges, ma'am?" the officer asked, eyeing my disheveled clothes and the beginnings of bruises around my neck and on my cheeks.

"No, just get him out of here," I told them.

The police pressed charges, causing George to stay in jail for two days. He attended anger management classes, domestic violence counseling and alcohol counseling. He lived away from home for six weeks and started coming to church with me. Optimistic, I let him come back home. As long as he was on probation, everything was great. I was at the hopeful stage that he could be happy if he quit drinking and taking drugs. Then I found out he was hiding his abuses from me. He started to drink and take drugs again. I confronted him, but he denied it.

"Do you honestly believe I wouldn't know?" I asked

not by chance

him when he denied it yet again.

"I'm not doing anything. I told you," he raged.

"I know better. I know what you're like on drugs, and what you're like off drugs. You are definitely on," I disagreed.

Finally, he gave up denying it, and I told him he couldn't smoke in the house. I had quit cold turkey when I surrendered my life to God, and the smell of the sweet-sour marijuana made me sick to my stomach, especially when he taunted me with it.

"Oh, doesn't this smell good? Wouldn't you want to have some? Oh, that's right. You don't do this anymore. You found Jesus," he sneered.

"That's right. I don't and I did," I replied calmly.

A month after I surrendered my life to Jesus, I felt someone touching me. I asked George if it was him, and he mumbled, "No, go back to sleep."

Still feeling the touch, I heard, "It is I. I have come to tell you that I have set you free from your life so I can bring others like you back to me." I woke up one minute before my alarm went off.

Talking to a Christian co-worker, she told me that I had heard from God. "He wants you to be a disciple," she said. That was the first time I know of God speaking to me.

Though I was free from the anger that had resided in me for years, I still condemned myself for all of the bad things I had done in my past.

I met with Carla from Two Rivers Church to walk me

there with me

through forgiveness. I counseled with God, asking him to reveal to me the roots of my unforgiving attitude, the trigger that I may not remember.

"Who do you forgive?" Carla asked me after prayer.

"I forgive my parents for their alcoholism. I forgive my brother-in-law for molesting me. I forgive my sister for severing our relationship. I forgive my first husband for his affair. I forgive George for the abuse," I told her.

"Who else do you forgive?" she asked.

I thought about that for a while. "There is no one else," I replied.

"Don't you forgive yourself?" she asked.

"I can't."

"Yes, you can. Speak it out."

"I can't."

"Repeat after me. I forgive myself for everything I have done in my life to displease you, Lord."

Reluctantly, I repeated after her. But that was just the beginning of my forgiveness of myself. I still work on that every day. Every day, I need to repeat: "Who I am today doesn't have to reflect on who I was in my past."

After living with George's continued drug use and alcoholism for another year and a half, and after the incident with Tom and the police, I realized that I needed to get my kids out of that environment and life. After much prayer, it wasn't until I felt peace about leaving that the kids and I moved out. Life has been so good since. I never thought of the consequences that taking drugs could have on my life, like possibly losing my kids or harming them

not by chance

mentally because they were inhaling the marijuana smoke secondhand.

Now, the people I talk to that knew me before can hear the peace in my voice. They tell me I am a different person than they remember, and it is the peace in my voice. Now, I have an identity, a purpose and even dreams. I am a witness to others through my actions. I tell them, "All you have to do is surrender your life to God, accept him into your life and recognize that he died for our sins."

God has kept the bad influences out of my life. I'm surrounded at work by fellow Christians, and I am able to participate in a daily devotional with them. I know that he was with me all along because some of the things I have done would have surely landed me in jail. I know he was with me all along because I never lost my children. Despite being a horrible mother to them at times, my kids have stood by me, didn't get angry with me and loved me anyway. I am thankful to God today. Once insecure, I am now secure in his love. Once filled with anger, I am now filled with peace. I thank my God that he makes that happen every single day.

finally seeing clearly
the story of gary whittington
written by bryan alaspa

I sat in the classroom staring blankly at the book in front of me. The words seemed to be swarming and swimming across the page instead of coming together into sentences. I strained my eyes.

What is wrong with me? I thought nervously.

No one else in my class seemed to have any problem reading. All around me pencils were scratching away furiously, like insects buzzing in the woods, while mine sat in my hand like some backstreet road kill. When other students were called on by the teacher to read out loud, they seemed to have no problem. But my own tongue was like some strange alien, lying in my mouth, completely unable to form the words.

"You're stupid!" the kids would yell every chance they could get. "You can't even read!"

In those words, I felt lost and alone. But more than anything, I felt invaluable and even worthless. I couldn't even read — what would I ever be able to contribute to the world?

***

I was born in a small town in Maryland. It was the kind of town where, during the winter, maybe 8,000 people roamed the streets. However, during the summer

not by chance

months, the population could explode to more than 300,000 souls. We were near the ocean, and beaches lined the outer edge of the town. It was a place where everyone knew everyone else. It was hard to keep secrets in a town where someone could crash a car on one side of town, make a phone call and find out the person being called on the opposite end of town had already heard about the accident.

My parents were young when they had me, and I didn't exactly come out easily. In fact, I am only 20 years younger than both of them. My parents certainly loved me, but being little more than children themselves, they really didn't understand what a child needed. I was always craving attention, and I needed more than most.

"Why can't you read this stuff?" I remember my mother asking me. "You're so smart, Gary. You just need to try harder."

At that time, dyslexia wasn't a word people used that often, if at all. Kids picked on me and wanted to know what was wrong with me. No one had an answer for me, and I didn't have an answer for them, either. Of course, my sister, who was a bit older than me, was an angel. She was the perfect child and performed wonderfully in school.

"You should just be more like your sister," my parents recited. "Look at how well she's doing."

I wanted to experience life. Outside my window was a beach. I felt the world calling to me. I wanted to be out under the sun instead of inside trying to read words that

finally seeing clearly

would never register. I couldn't focus, and no one could understand that. I had trouble communicating with my friends and those my age. I couldn't understand why. It was probably inevitable that I would start to rebel. My parents were trying to run a small business and had little time to spend with me. I wanted attention. If that meant I had to throw things around or create trouble to get it, then that was fine by me. I never hurt anyone, and I never tried any drugs, but I couldn't concentrate to do my work. School was an endless agony for me.

I remember spending numerous days staring at the papers in front of me. It felt like the teacher was always standing right behind me, pushing me, prodding me, while I stared at my desk, wishing with all my might I could just disappear into the grains. Around me, it felt like the kids were all laughing, glancing over with smirks that could make even the class president feel ashamed. I failed test after test, and my self-worth dropped notch after notch.

Across the table from me, at dinner, there was my sister. She was getting high grades and passing everything so easily.

"See how she does it?" my mother would ask me. "If you just buckled down like your sister does, you could get better grades, too."

She was trying to encourage me. I knew that even then, but I couldn't do what she was asking. I tried so hard. However, I wanted to run, to explore the world. My mind was always working a million miles a minute. It was like

not by chance

having a radio stuck between stations in my brain. My brain was always filled with static from too much input and information from outside fighting to get in. Whatever natural filters the rest of my class, and my sister, may have had were absent from my distracted brain. I felt like an outcast.

"I'll help you study," my teacher told me back in second grade. "Your mother asked me to stay after school with you. We'll look over the lessons together."

So there I would sit, more time spent in a classroom. Outside, through the windows, my schoolmates would be playing and yelling in the sunshine. My soul ached to be out there with them. The teacher would sit behind me and review each and every lesson with me. That would go on for hours before my mother would come and pick me up.

"We'll study together," she would tell me, as she shuffled around in her purse to find the keys to our family car. "When we get home, we'll have dinner, and then we'll study for your test tomorrow."

So, instead of going out and playing when I got home, I would sit with my mother and reread what I had spent hours reading with the teacher. I would try hard to remember each sentence and each word. We would study every question and every note. I would memorize and repeat and then do it again. Facts jumbled in my head as the sun slowly set behind the horizon. As I fell asleep, the words and facts became a noise in my head that melted into the background of my life.

The next morning, I shuffled into school. My hands

finally seeing clearly

were slick with sweat. I sat down at the desk and tried to remain positive.

"You studied," I told myself. "You know this. You can do it."

I just couldn't quite get myself to believe those words. The test slid across my desk, and my mouth went dry. My thoughts froze. The pencil shook between my fingers. It was like looking at a text in a foreign language. I couldn't remember anything. The words swam together into gibberish, and my eyes nearly welled with tears as that soreness that creeps up your throat just before a wailing sob latched onto my vocal cords and held tight. It felt miserable.

As usual, I ended up failing again.

"Next time, you'll have to study harder," the teacher would say.

"Next time, we'll stay up until you really know it all," my mother would encourage.

***

At 13 years old, I became active within our church. My family was Episcopalian, and I became an altar boy. I went to church every Sunday. I sat with the Bible open in front of me as I listened to the stories and the scripture. Here was a huge, thick book filled with words and no pictures. Inside of it, so I was told, was everything I needed to know about how to live my life. However, to me, it was just a swimming, churning jumble of words with no meaning.

not by chance

How could God have the answers to my life and not present it in a form that I could understand? I wanted my life to have meaning. I wanted a life that would make me feel free and worthwhile, and here it was at my fingertips, but I couldn't reach it.

I talked to the older men in the congregation and listened to their stories. None of it connected with me, however. I felt a great distance between me and this being who created me. Soon, it was my time to be confirmed, but I just went through the motions of confirmation. Something about those Jesus stories wasn't connecting with me.

At the time, I just wasn't ready to respect the scripture that was being read to me. It probably also didn't help that my dyslexia prevented me from understanding them. I just became more frustrated. I prayed about it, because that was what I was told to do. Going to church every Sunday created a habit of prayer in me, and I prayed every night. I prayed every week while in that pew in church. I waited, eagerly, hoping to hear something back. What would a sign look like?

I never did receive one.

I started praying less and less. I lost touch with the church I had been attending my entire life until that point. All of that praying and studying just started to seem like a waste of time to me. Of course, this was mostly because I struggled to understand it and couldn't read enough to learn anything on my own. So I put this idea of God on the backburner of my life and continued in my search for value, self-worth and purpose. I was going to do this my-

finally seeing clearly

self.

I struggled through the final years of grade school and then moved on to high school. It was there that I finally found something to focus my attention on.

I got involved in athletics. I started playing soccer and lacrosse. I discovered self-worth. When it came to activities, with me, I was either always completely focused on what I was doing or completely distracted. Therefore, once I got involved in athletics, I put all of my energy into them. I committed to them fully.

"Maybe you aren't as dumb as you looked," I remember friends who had made fun of me once saying, once I entered high school.

My classes turned around. I started to buckle down and concentrate. I had gained a feeling of self-worth through my athletic activities, and that gave me the courage to dedicate myself to my classes. I learned how to live with my dyslexia and learned how to read. It was never effortless, but I was finally able to read the papers and passages that teachers placed in front of me more easily. I was also now able to retain things I had read. It was difficult, and I studied more than most others, but I managed to get past it.

With this new confidence and better performance both in school and out of it, I was feeling better about me. I was getting the attention I had always craved. I felt valuable, maybe even worth something. Not only was I doing well in class, but I decided to run for student president. Not only did I run, but I won. Now I was in charge of

not by chance

things, which created a new responsibility for me. People listened to me. I began to be inspiring to others.

"Why can't I be like everyone else?" I remember asking before I entered high school. Life had been beyond predatory before that time and before I found athletics.

"Why does everyone have to put me down?"

"They make fun of what they don't understand," my mother would tell me. At the same time, she was pleading with me to focus and do better.

Now I was, but my sister was moving in the opposite direction. She was going through a rebellious phase in college. While I was student president, she was failing her classes and running out to party.

My sister sank into alcohol and drugs. I was not prepared to be of any help. I was still struggling with my life and disabilities. Things were going well, but I had to work harder than most people. As my sister partied all night, I was studying. I wore a tie to parties and didn't drink. We were polar opposites, as it turned out.

My parents would argue with her on the phone, threatening her that they would take her out of college if she didn't straighten herself out. She turned to me.

"Gary, help me out here. I helped you before."

When I didn't, she took it out on me. I seethed back at her, but I didn't retaliate. I just let that anger fester for a while.

I managed to obtain a job during the summer. Now I had money for myself. I was still struggling with what I wanted to do with my life. All the people around me, as

finally seeing clearly

they grew older and college loomed in front of them, seemed to know what they wanted to do and where they wanted to go. Not me; I was still just wishing I could read the morning newspaper with ease.

Though I felt more valuable, I still didn't feel like I had a purpose. Yes, I was good at athletics, and yes, I could actually now pass a class. And you could yell "Mr. President" down the high school hallway and see me smile in return. But that sense of life purpose, the kind that instills value deeper than the value other people assign you, was still missing from my life.

Then came the day I found art. It was like the heavens opened before me, smiled and presented my first art class on a silver platter. I knew I was home. When there was a pencil in my hand or a piece of clay for me to form, I was in a place that I just knew was familiar. It was like being with an old friend or a long-lost relative. I could mold an entire world with my own hands. I had absolute freedom.

Soon, I began experimenting with every part of what art is. I covered my fingers with dust from colored pencils and pastels. I covered my clothes with paint. I buried my hands and arms in clay. I spent hour after hour working with whatever form of art I was interested in at that time. I was amazed as it seemed like I could slowly mold, shape and manipulate the entire world with my fingers. When I got involved in my art, time and space didn't matter to me. The world fell away. Whatever problems I may have had disappeared. With art, I could communicate with the world, and I didn't have to worry about words getting in

not by chance

the way.

As it was with everything in my life, once I discovered art, I became obsessed with it. I threw myself into it. To me, there was nothing else going on anywhere in the world. Athletics even fell by the wayside. It had to; I couldn't be pulled in too many directions. The only thing I wanted to do was create works of art.

As the years flew by in high school and college loomed, the prospect of going to art school rose before my eyes. It would mean shaking up my world and moving to a new place, but it would also mean being surrounded by art.

Nothing could send me down a spiral of confusion and dismay faster than changing my environment. I chose a school that would develop me as an artist — an 18-hour drive away, where I didn't know a single person. I knew I'd learn more about art, but I feared everything else it entailed, even on the emotional level.

I attended Interlocken Arts Academy, in northern Michigan. I remember the moment I first stood on the green campus grounds. All around me were younger students and their families, kids of all ages from all around the country. Each of them had a purpose, or thought they did. It was a campus full of life and music and expression.

Now, I had graduated high school in Maryland that year, so deciding to return to another in the fall was out of the norm. My friends back home thought I had lost it again. "Go ahead, Gary, see you in 20," they would joke.

As I feared, the sudden change sent my life and emo-

finally seeing clearly

tions into upheaval. I knew no one. I retreated from the world when it came to people, but I threw myself into my studies. I was the first person in the history of the school to attend for two post-graduate years. I took everything. I took every class I could get my hands on, so to speak.

That first year was about getting grounded. I had to get my feet under me. There were many nights when I would sit alone in my room and cry myself to sleep. The other students around me seemed to adjust perfectly, but I was struggling. I would call home every chance I got.

"I need to come home," I cried to my mother, while huddling in a corner so no one else could hear me.

"You just need to give it time," she would reply. "You can do this."

"I can't stand it here anymore," I cried, this time louder and caring less about who heard me.

"Calm down," she stated coolly back to me. "Just focus on your studies. Before you know it, the end of the year will be here."

I still didn't put an emphasis on God in my life on a regular basis. I knew he was there, but I didn't spend much time thinking about him or praying to him. I dropped those habits with my altar boy cloak many years ago. Even so, I felt that he was somehow strangely leading me to places I would have never gone without his unique and gentle guidance.

Somewhere in my college years, I started to show an interest in members of the opposite sex. For me, however, there were either relationships or there was art. There was

not by chance

little in between. However, there was no denying the standard feelings and hormones that came with being that age and surrounded by women.

The first time I asked out a woman was like something out of a movie. My knees shook as though the floor were heaving beneath me from some terrible earthquake. My mouth was dry. I thought my heart would burst right out of my chest and fall on the floor between us like a dying, flapping fish. Words had always failed me in the past. Why did I think they wouldn't fail me this time?

"So, I was wondering," I managed at last, "would you maybe like to get something to eat or go see a movie this weekend?"

To my everlasting surprise and shock, she smiled and softly replied, "Yeah, I'd love to."

So, I entered a relationship with a woman. She was my first girlfriend. While others my age were looking for sexual intimacy, for me, it was just amazing that this person wanted to spend any time with me at all. I felt like I was on top of the world. Just holding her hand was enough to make me understand that there was a God in his heaven and that Jesus was real.

Still, I struggled with relationships. It was tough for me to meet people. I was naturally shy. Whenever I walked into a new place, I could hear those children from my childhood laughing at me.

"You're stupid!" I would hear them yelling in my mind.

"You're never going to amount to anything!" I heard

finally seeing clearly

from another voice, calling from the distant past.

When I was in a relationship, it was hard for me to divide my time. It took so much of my concentration to communicate, to make my art and to study, it was hard to find time for this other person in my life. At the same time, when I wanted to focus just on that person, my studies would suffer.

"I need you to spend time with me," I remember one girl asking me. "You've always got your nose to some piece of paper or your hands buried in a lump of clay. What about me?"

"Art is what I am," I replied. "It's what makes me who I am. It's the only thing that makes sense to me."

"I thought I made sense to you," she replied with a sigh and tears standing out like stars against her irises.

During my second year, I got involved with another woman. I was very much in love, but it turned out that she wasn't nearly as in love with me. While I was out buying her flowers, arranging romantic dinners or creating artwork dedicated to her name, she was busy looking around for something else. I was ready to make my life all about her and dedicate myself to her. Apparently, she was busy making plans to be with anyone else.

At some point, when you are holding a conversation with someone, and it is obvious that she isn't listening or caring about what you're saying, you start to get the hint. She ended up breaking my heart, however, when it became very obvious she wasn't in love with me like I was in love with her. I was devastated, and my heart was heavy. I

not by chance

retired to my room, alone in the dark, and resolved to make a change in my life and for the remainder of that year.

"Give up on women and relationships," I declared to myself once it happened. "You need to just give up on women and relationships."

My heart was pained, but I threw myself back into my art and my schoolwork. I focused past the women who walked by me and sat in class with me daily. I was into my artwork and my schoolwork 100 percent. I graduated with honors that year.

My mother, father and grandmother came to see me when I graduated. They had visited the school for the first time to support me and show me that they were proud of me. While I was not an enemy to my father, I was always closest to my mother and grandmother. In a lot of ways, we were like the Three Musketeers as I grew up.

"I told you that you could do it," my mother told me, as I stood there in my graduation best.

"I know you did," I whispered back to her. "I just needed to believe it myself. Now I do."

It was time to go to Cleveland and start it all over again. I wanted to continue to study art, and Cleveland boasted a university that offered a five-year program. I knew when it came to art, I wanted to specialize in sculpture.

Once again, though, I found myself dividing my time between artwork, schoolwork and relationships. I got involved with a woman, and she ended up being abusive. It

finally seeing clearly

wasn't physical abuse, it was all verbal abuse. Nothing I did for her was right. Whatever I did, she wanted me to do it again or she would do it for me. She insulted me. She reminded me of the kids who called me stupid when I was a child. She would lead me on, convincing me that she was completely in love with me. One moment she would be dedicated to me, the next she would act like she didn't want to see me again. She played mind games with me.

It left me devastated, and I wanted to go home for a while. I moved back to Maryland.

"What are you doing home?" I remember my mother asking me.

"It's nothing," I replied, not wanting to tell her what had happened. "I just needed a bit of a break."

Even though I'd gained confidence through my experiences with athletics and art in high school and college, I was still seeking self-worth. I was still that kid who had to try harder than all the others, still that kid in the elementary school classroom who felt that the world around him didn't see him for the bright student he was. Now, I was the kid who couldn't hold a relationship and who failed at holding a romance at all. I was still looking for something that would make me feel like I mattered. I was still seeking something that would make me feel complete.

I went back to school, tried hard to forget about my relationship and threw myself back into work. Graduation finally arrived, and suddenly, the rest of the world loomed before me. I was still hurting from my last relationship and sank in and out of depressions. There were times

not by chance

when I didn't even want to go on.

I discovered massage therapy while I was going to school and in the years after it, researched the idea more. My mother ran a nail salon, and I spent time as a nail technician in her salon, but I knew that wasn't something I wanted to do for the rest of my life.

However, I saw how well the women loved to be touched and massaged when they went to the spa. I thought that would be a way to experience the contact I needed. There's nothing greater than a woman's compliment when you truly make her feel feminine and beautiful.

As I sat there polishing and trimming women's nails, I was quiet. I was still uncomfortable talking to women. I withdrew into myself. Women had chewed me up and spat me out, and I just didn't want to get involved again with any of them.

I wanted to find someone who would love me unconditionally. I also wanted to be able to love someone unconditionally. This seemed almost impossible to find. But sometimes, God works miracles even for unconfident, lowly guys like me.

I met a woman who was Catholic, strictly by chance. It was just one of those things where I was out one night, locked eyes with a woman across the room and approached her to talk.

"Hi, I'm Gary," I said to her. My lines hadn't really gotten any better all these years later.

"Nice to meet you, Gary," she said with a smile. I was

finally seeing clearly

amazed that anyone would respond to me.

Before I knew it, we were spending time talking on the phone and making plans to see each other. I fell in love. I thought this was the thing that I was meant to find. I thought this was the relationship that I was meant to have for the rest of my life.

"I'll be with you forever," I spoke softly in her ear.

"I need you to convert to my faith," was her reply.

So, I started the process of converting to Catholicism. I loved her, and I wanted to do whatever it took to marry her. I took the classes and studied. Once again, I had thrown myself utterly into a relationship. We were married in a Catholic church after being together for four years.

We tried to make our marriage work for three years, while I studied to be a massage therapist. We didn't have any children, but things were tense between us. I didn't feel right at the Catholic services. I knew it wasn't right for me. The divide between us began to grow as the years progressed. In some ways, I felt like our Catholic church was trying to control people, and that never sat well with me.

As my marriage began to fall apart, I began to pray. I had learned how to pray when I was a child, sitting in those pews, surrounded by older men who seemed to understand what was going on. Over the years, my habit of praying had fallen by the wayside. All of the classes I had taken to convert to Catholicism reminded me of the power of prayer. I tapped into those old memories of how to pray as I stood in my house.

not by chance

I remember staring out the window of my home, my wife elsewhere in the house, as the sun set and turned the sky into a dazzling array of colors and praying. I was praying for direction. I was praying for strength. I knew that either I had to focus all of my attention into making this marriage work or I had to get out.

"I am so sorry," I told my wife after my quiet time. "We can't do this anymore."

"Then I need you to get an annulment," she told me with tears in her eyes.

Once again, I beheld a failed relationship before me and a woman in tears in front of me.

I went through with the annulment. I was at an all-time low. However, I had the feeling that there was more going on in my life than just me. Once again, those feelings of having no self-worth returned to me, this time, like a poison, invading my veins and weakening me to my knees. I had failed again. I was feeling as stupid and worthless, again, as everyone had always told me I would feel. I felt disconnected from everyone, all over again.

I had been praying against the window, staring at the sunset and wondering about the world. I wondered what turned a man to evil in his life. Suddenly, I understood how easy it could be for a man to turn to evil. It was like I heard a voice in my head.

"What do you want to do with your life?" it asked me. "Do you want to kill someone? Do you want to steal? Or do you want to have real relationships? Do you want to trust me and where I am going to take you? Do you want

finally seeing clearly

to find value?"

I moved back home, and I knew I had nothing. I had no wife. I had no job. I had no confidence, no personally assigned value. It was in those moments of nothingness that I finally opened myself up to God, not like I had as an altar boy where I listened cynically and dismissed the Jesus stories quickly. This time, I turned my face to him and told him to do with me what he wanted. I asked for help. I put myself in his hands and literally gave up control of my quickly crumbling life.

In that moment, I gave my life to God for the first time.

As if to say, "Finally!" it was then that God brought me the woman who would change my life and my idea of love and value forever.

Just as I had begun to feel God's presence in my life, I felt the world revolve beneath me when I first saw her. I had learned how to become a massage therapist by that time, and she was a massage therapist, as well. Once again, I tried out one of my shy lines on her, but this time, it worked.

Before I knew it, we were together. The problem was, of course, that she was from a place far away from where I was. In order to make our life work, I would have to move to Phoenix, Arizona. Everyone thought I was crazy.

"What are you doing?" I remember my cousin asking me. "You know you haven't had the best of luck with women. You don't know this woman. Why are you moving so far away just for a woman?"

not by chance

"I'm trusting that this is what God wants me to do," I told him. "He wants me to be with this person, and I know it."

I felt it in my bones. It's hard for me to explain it better than that. I just knew that God was working in my life. I had some idea of what the clay felt like when I was being molded and shaped by his hands. I felt his giant hands were guiding me and my life. I just knew that where I was going was where God wanted me to be. I knew it just like I knew the sky, during the summer months, was blue and that the stars were bright at night. It was a certainty that I'd never felt before that moment that I gave my life up to him.

I met my wife in October, moved to Phoenix in January and was engaged to her by February. Yes, you could say we moved rather quickly, but God's signs were irrefutable.

My wife came from a family with two parents who had struggled with alcoholism. As such, she had been coping for some time with her own demons. I knew, without a doubt, as if God himself had tapped me on the head, that this was why I was here. I was here to be with her to help her with her demons. I knew that by doing that, I would conquer any of my demons still left.

I started working in a resort as a massage therapist. Every day I touched naked women, and I dealt with those demons to remain professional. My wife and I experienced our struggles, but we got through them together. I finally saw the signs God had given to me and God, in turn, pro-

finally seeing clearly

vided.

Paralleled with our growth as a couple, we were in conflict to find community. We had no family near us and a handful of close friends to lean on. We had gone from church to church with no luck trying to find a true fit. We prayed together, asking for what we wanted. Then, in God's guidance and help from a young couple we were acquainted with, we found what we had been craving — a wonderful newly developed Christian community having services in an elementary school cafeteria. Two Rivers was the church for us.

At that point, our relationship with God was struggling with uncertainty. Within two months of attending services regularly together, in the middle of a little cafeteria at Two Rivers, we asked for God's help and together, we were born again.

Being "born again" means that we decided to ask God to give us new life, this time, in him. We asked God to come into our hearts and to forgive us of all our past sins. That day, we accepted Jesus Christ as our Savior, and we embraced the new life that new birth invites.

"You could not have been more ready," the pastor replied confidently, as he gazed into our eyes. Together in unity, the Holy Spirit took over our lives, and we ached with relief.

Not long after, a woman I had been helping for many months by kneading away her aches and pains asked me about my life. I told her about how I was also an artist and that I had always dreamed of making art for a living. I also

not by chance

told her that, financially speaking, this was just not feasible for me. Both my wife and I had to work to make ends meet. There were just not enough hours in the day to make ends meet and still make art.

"Gary," she supposed, "you've done so much to help me. You've done so much to make me feel good, I want to help you. I want to sponsor you. My husband and I have money, and we want to sponsor you so you can make your art."

Not only was I blessed to be able to make my art, something that always seemed just out of my feasible reach, but I was soon blessed with a child. I was 40 years old, my wife was 39, and yet, we were blessed with a son.

All it took for those blessings to come raining down was that moment, that blessed moment, when I opened myself up to God and then accepted his son, Jesus, to be my Savior. As soon as I realized that my life was his and opened my soul up to him, the blessings began to flow. Has it always been easy? Not at all. I face challenges every single day. I worry about focusing too much on my art and balancing that with being a husband and father, too.

I just know that I am doing what God wants me to do. I know that I am creating art that will glorify him. I know that, wherever I go and whatever obstacles come my way, God is guiding me. He blesses me every day.

I no longer feel like I am worthless. I am a father and a husband. More than anything, I am loved and needed. People don't care whether or not I can read a test, but they do care that I can provide for them, make beauty for them

finally seeing clearly

and teach them through my art to appreciate the world's beauty I now see so clearly.

With God's help, art is my contribution to the world, the contribution my grade school self never dreamed possible. There is no greater feeling of worth than that. That kind of worth comes directly from Christ alone.

home
the story of jill kindervater
written by christee wise

Once again, I drew the jagged car key across my flesh, feeling the unexplainable relief of drawing my own blood with its cold edge. As warm, red drops oozed and trickled down the inside of my lower left leg, I closed my eyes and embraced the sense of peace that was coming over me. The blood that flowed was tears I needed to shed but could not cry. I had found my release. Mildly conscious of the external pain, I saw it as just punishment for losing my best friend. The mutilation of my flesh was a blessed distraction from the unbearable grief and rejection in my tormented heart. Again and again, I sliced with mounting satisfaction that the blood I spilled on the carpet would leave a stain my mother would have to work into her decorating scheme for *my* house. The ugly scenes with Hannah and Mother were now tightly pressed together, and *I* was back in control.

***

My 18th birthday not long before was to have been my Independence Day. 18 was the magic number I'd been counting on for months, even years. Tension with my parents had reached the boiling point, and even they agreed I should be on my own. They had helped me purchase a mobile home not far from them in the little town of

not by chance

Wheatland, Wyoming. Even though no one can live very far from anyone else in such a tiny town, I was ecstatic at the thought of being free of the smothering attention of my parents. Resentment simmered below the surface every day of my teenaged life as I studied alone, went to church alone, dreamed alone, struggled alone and searched alone for some sense of identity. My ray of hope was to move away from the isolation when I turned 18 and together with my best friend, determine my own path.

"Now, Jill. Having your own place doesn't mean you can do whatever you want," my parents cautioned. "As long as we are helping you, there are still some rules." Those rules included a curfew, strict restrictions on guests, no overnight company and the fact that they would decide how I could decorate the place.

It took all my resolve to keep from exploding, "I'm 18. I'm moving out. I'm done with you!"

The hope that kept me going had grown bright and then faded when my friendship with Hannah had dissolved the previous year. Had we still been best friends, we'd be making plans together and supporting one another in the battle for independence. Still carrying the heartbreak and uncertainty of her rejection, I struggled now to reassemble scraps of self-worth and confidence I needed to pursue finding myself and my way.

"I've got to get out," I told myself, "no matter what rules they put on me."

My determination lasted about as long as it took Mom to travel to Cheyenne and bring home wallpaper samples.

home

"Stay calm, keep cool," I coached myself, as my mother and I assessed the samples sitting out on our kitchen table. I'd have been thankful to have that counter swallow them all rather than spewing them before us, as it was doing now. I was *not* in favor of wallpaper at all for my house. But I sat down beside my mother and dutifully began to flip the pages, trying to muster up some enthusiasm to imagine the possibilities.

"Here, Jill, isn't this one pretty?" my mother bubbled.

"I guess so. How much is it?"

"Well, I don't know." We crunched the numbers.

"Mom, why are we looking at $100 wallpaper? Why can't I just paint my bedroom?" I responded, now sitting at my computer where I could take some breathing space from the hundreds of samples before me. My favorite game blurred across the screen as a distraction from my wallpaper-crazed mother.

In my head, I had a vision of what I wanted — an Arabian sort of style with red roses and gold leafing. In my mind, it was gorgeous. "That way, I can get the exact color I want and sponge on some roses or accents in red and gold."

Mother closed the book with a slam that made me jump. I could see she was angry. I knew I was. It seemed like we'd been like this forever, always fighting, never agreeing. Everything became an argument. We'd been in a four-year tug of war of the wills. Both of us were tired of it, but we were both too stubborn to give up.

Mother spat, "If you don't like it, don't tell me to be

not by chance

quiet. Why don't you just move out?"

I spit back, "Fine!"

That night, I began cutting myself, and the next day, I moved from that house to another on my own.

This wasn't at all where I expected to be after graduating high school and turning 18. Trying to seize control of my life, I watched helplessly as it spun out of control instead.

"I hate you, God."

It wasn't the first time I'd said it. God was about power, and in my opinion, he hadn't handled it very responsibly in my life.

***

I grew up in the best place on earth. Adopted at 6 months by a retired marine and his wife, I was their only child. Homeschooled my entire life, my world was our 80-acre ranch in the flat Wyoming plains. The Laramie Mountains rose up in the distance as mighty guardians of my paradise. Wooded creek beds mischievously broke loose from the square pattern of endless open fields. Ranch life itself was a perfect balance between the routine of chores and the freedom to ride, play and explore with the animals. I knew no rejection, only the unconditional love of horses, cattle, cats, dogs and even a goat my father bought me one year at the state fair. We had every farm animal, except pigs and chickens.

"I love you, Penny." I wrapped my arms around the

home

neck of my best friend, a 7-year-old copper and white painted mare. She was huge and magnificent, but I'd never been afraid of her. Penny let me brush her till she shone like copper coins on a satiny, white wedding dress. As I reached up in invitation, she bent her head down so that I could look into her enormous brown eyes. It was like looking into a mirror. She had a wild and free spirit like me.

"You're a beautiful lady," I told her. She shook her head gently to say she'd had enough affection and was ready to move. I was game, enjoying her company more than anything else on earth. I belonged to her, she belonged to me, and we belonged here.

Today I chose not to use the blanket and saddle but simply climbed onto her painted bare back and let her lead the way. Penny was a mysterious wonder to me. She required a firm hand. Yet, she was so quick to respond to the rein. She gave a ride so smooth you couldn't even tell you were on her. She seemed unaware that the stalls and the barn and the fences were boundaries to be tested. Maybe they were so widely spaced that she was content to roam within their bounds. Perhaps she understood how much I adored her and that to lose her would break my heart.

***

On Sundays, we went to church in town. This was my main social connection, as it seemed to be for almost all of Wheatland. Most everyone attended church in Wheat-

not by chance

land. There were 20 churches of all different forms and faiths in the town of 3,500. The majority, though, were Baptist of one kind or another, and our family attended one of them.

My first real human friendship came when I was about 7 or 8 years old. I began taking violin lessons from a local musician who ran a shop in a strip mall. She had a daughter close to my age, and we soon became friends. It wasn't long before I accepted an invitation to Sunday school with her and eventually began to attend their fundamentalist church. Seeing that I was planted, my parents stopped attending church shortly after but insisted that I continue to be there regularly.

The rhythm of my days was set, and I found comfort in the steady canter. Everything made sense and was dependable. I tagged along with Dad, baling hay and moving irrigation pipe. From my mother, I learned to read and cook. There was never an idle moment, for when free time arose, I shared it with Penny in sunshine or snow.

***

"Jill, we're selling the farm and moving into town."

The announcement came out of the blue one day when I was 13. I could not have been more shocked and hurt had Penny thrown me to the rock-hard ground and trampled me. Nor could I have felt more helpless. Nothing had prepared me for this betrayal. Even beyond that, something that had happened many years before prevented my

home

heart from absorbing and expressing the sadness that now poured into it.

One day when I was just 5, I had hurt myself in the barn and began to cry really hard. My father was beside me in two strides. But he was awkward about my outburst. He quickly assessed the damage as not fatal and commanded, "Now, Jill, you're a marine's daughter. Marines don't cry. Be a marine, and stop that crying." Eager to please, I smeared the tears away, leaving dirty streaks across my face. I subconsciously vowed to meet his expectation. In the years that followed, I collected enough instances like this one that I soon refined the art of controlling my tears — an art I employed as all explanation my parents gave for the decision to leave the beautiful ranch was lost on me. In that moment, I needed desperately to grieve the loss of my world. Instead, I was struck dumb with shock and the conditioning I had not to cry. I could not summon the appropriate emotion. I spent the next few weeks in a daze as we prepared to move. Inwardly, I raged, "Why, God?"

Dust rolled up around the pickup as we pulled out of the driveway for the last time. I couldn't lift my hand to roll up the window. I was choking with grief and blind with rage. At that moment, I locked the gate of my heart.

And I told God that I hated him.

Moving to town did not diminish my isolation. Without the hum of the farm, I was completely lost. My life was home and church. I hated both. At home, there were far fewer chores than on the farm, and they were far less in-

not by chance

teresting. Then we moved several times to different houses. My dad thought it would be great to sell everything we owned, buy an MCI coach motor home and travel all over the country, staying in KOA campgrounds. We wound up spending a whole year parked in a lot in Wyoming, walking everywhere. Finally, we bought another house. During this time, I role-played the dutiful daughter, deciding not to put my parents through the torture I saw in families where rebellious teenagers wreaked havoc. I continued to attend youth activities at church, only because it was expected. Even when I was there, I simply conformed to the expectations, providing the correct responses and earning the merit badges. My resentment grew weekly as did the impossibly long list of do's and don'ts I learned in Sunday school and Bible club. All this time, I was trying to please everyone, and loneliness and anger threatened like monsters to swallow me alive.

"Who am I? Where do I fit?" Typical questions of a typical teenager overwhelmed me. Since I was alone most of the hours of most of my days, there was no one to ask. In desperation, I begged God for a best friend.

As I pled with an uncaring God for the warmth of human relationship, I found escape and connection online. Role-play in the E-world rewards the gamer with power and control. Online, I had access to more friends than I ever dreamed were in or out of Wheatland. I also had control. *Runescape*, a medieval-themed fantasy, became my favorite game. In my character, *Cleocatrah,* I became someone who managed her adventurous life with grace

home

and skill. I floated away from my isolation for hours on my imagination, chatting away with dozens of other real souls wearing imaginary characters. All the while, my parents thought I was happily playing computer games by myself. And what I could hide, I could control.

Getting a job held several attractions. It was definitely a step toward independence; it was also something to do outside of home, school and church, and I'd meet people. As soon as I was old enough, I got a job at *Terragrano*. This little mom and pop restaurant was an Italian bistro in our small town. We served pizza, salads and sandwiches, and we had an espresso bar. It was nice to meet a variety of people, and I became pretty good friends with my boss, Sheri. It eased my boredom and some of my loneliness.

***

Hannah came along after I'd long given up praying for a best friend. In spite of that, I couldn't help thanking God for the answer. At 16, we came to know each other at a time when both of us needed a friend. Hannah and I were complete opposites and much alike at the same time. I was tall, she was tiny. She had blond hair and a pale complexion. I had auburn hair and darker features. She considered herself a "skater" or "stoner chick." I leaned toward a gothic, renaissance style. We both were trying to find our identity and to fit in. Raised as good, church-going girls, both of us were more than ready to push the limits. By this time, I had a car and some spending money and plenty of

not by chance

time to use them. We became an inseparable pair, looking for fun. We often found trouble. The friendship took the fear out of our penchant for testing boundaries.

Then I was doubly blessed.

"My name is Racquel, what's yours?" she asked, and I felt flattered that she seemed interested in me. We'd struck up a conversation as I waited on her one day at the restaurant. Even though she was just a couple years older than me, I was impressed by her confidence. She possessed self-assurance, along with flair and style I admired. It wasn't hard, then, for her to pique my interest in Wicca.

Racquel took me under her wing and showed me the ropes. "Explore, experiment and embrace" were steps on the path to power, I learned. I began to study, read about and research this white witchcraft which promised the ability to make my life easy, and, if I desired, to make it hard for other people. Convinced that I would be a responsible custodian once I had it, I set out on a quest for power, intending only to use it for good. The secret thought of ultimately having divine power of life and death in my hands was certainly enticing.

That Wicca was not my parents' religion was no small factor in the temptation, either. It delivered more power than I'd seen in any religion so far. When I began to realize the power of making things I wanted to happen, I was eager to share it with Hannah.

"Do you know what this means?" I finally blurted after a 10-minute monologue about tarot readings and spells. We were sitting in a local Chinese restaurant, enjoying

home

some soft drinks after work one summer evening.

"What?" She was less than enthusiastic.

"We can *make* our parents let us get an apartment."

She fiddled with her straw. I couldn't believe she wasn't as excited as I was.

"C'mon, it's so sweet! I'm seeing things and doing things and controlling things I've never done before. I'll introduce you to Racquel, and she can explain it better," I suggested.

But she declined, and after that, I didn't try to bring her into it again. At the same time, I didn't hide it from her. I figured she'd become interested if I didn't push.

***

A few weeks later, Hannah called.

"Meet me at the park. We need to talk." Her voice sounded flat as I picked up the phone. We no longer needed to identify ourselves when we called one another. We were best friends.

"So, Han, what's up?" I pulled the car to a shady area of the park where she'd been waiting. She climbed in beside me, holding a Bible in her lap. It was odd to see her with it. I felt a strange sense of calm, though, while she was obviously uncomfortable. She fanned the pages nervously, keeping her eyes down away from mine.

"It... It... It's just not right, Jill," she started in a hushed, fearful tone.

"What's not right?" I demanded.

not by chance

"This witch stuff, it... it's evil."

"What are you talking about?" I was on the defense. "It's just for fun. Gettin' what we want for a change instead of what everybody else tells us we need."

"It just feels evil," she swallowed. Her eyes were tearing up, and I was worried she was starting to freak out.

"Look," I tried to calm her down, "I'm not worshipping Satan or anything. I just want to get what I want sometimes, instead of doing what everyone else tells me I should do."

"Yes, but it's really creepin' me out. Something's really wrong." Her hand shook as she started to look for something in the Bible, so unused that it still looked brand new.

"Hey, don't be getting all religious on me. This is just something to have fun with. C'mon, girl, it's just a game."

"No, Jill, it's not a game." She was beginning to break down. "It's really dangerous. I can feel it. It's evil." She forced herself to look at me.

"What are you saying? I'm not going to let you take this away from me. There's nothing wrong with it. I've finally got some power to know what's going to happen, to control things in my life. I'm not going to let anything bad happen to you. Listen, I've got these two protectors, Trevor and Clarissa. They're not going to let anything happen to us."

"But you know it's against the Bible," she urged.

I almost laughed. "That's ridiculous. As long as what we're doing is for our good and we're doing it with an open heart, to help people, it's not Satan worship. I have

home

control of it, don't you see?"

As I said this, I noticed that the clouds were moving irregularly in the sky. Hannah closed her eyes, shook her head and put it down, as though she could shake off some oppressive force.

I didn't feel it. I couldn't understand why she was so upset. She sounded panicked, almost shrieking, "No, no, this is bad, really bad. I'm scared, Jill. Make it stop." Goosebumps were now appearing on her arms. I didn't know she could be any paler, but she had no color whatsoever in her face as she leaned her head back against the seat. Her eyes did not open.

"It just feels evil, like dark and cold," she moaned. Her arms were now crossed in front of her, and she was holding herself tightly and swaying a little in the seat.

The sky continued to roll and move. It was still clear, but it was turning dark. "It's like death," Hannah went on, her voice sounding almost terrified. "It's all around, and it's pulling me in."

From blue to black to sulfurous yellow-green, the sky swirled before me. I had never seen these colors. Out of the soup of the sky emerged shapes, skeletons and ghastly figures, icy, faceless personifications of death and emptiness that sucked life from human presence. I was seeing what Hannah was feeling.

Even as I experienced the darkness, I felt some pleasure that I had reached out to touch new levels of the spiritual world. For Hannah, though, I was afraid. I leapt out of the car and began calling to the gods to back off. I turned

not by chance

in a circle on the grass with my arms and hands slightly lifted. I didn't know who I was talking to, so I addressed the powers surrounding me on all sides. I said, "You have me, just leave her alone."

Hannah was sobbing and clutching the Bible when I got back in the car. When her eyes opened, they were wide with fear as she looked at me.

"You're gonna stop, right? I mean, I feel like I don't know you anymore."

"I'm fine. And so are you. Everything is going to be fine," I said, as much to myself about our friendship as to her about the witchcraft. Uncertainty suddenly filled me as I watched her leave. She didn't call for a week. In a matter of weeks, Hannah became angry about something else, and I never heard from her again. There was nothing for me to do but blame myself for having opened my big mouth and scaring my first — and only — best friend away.

***

Moving out totally on my own allowed me to explore witchcraft more freely. I set up a corner in my house where I would light candles to the god and goddess. Different colors represented various ways of thought. I spent hours studying and researching. A practicing witch is what I began to call myself. To be a full-fledged witch, I would need much more study and a chance to build up my power.

home

At the same time, in secrecy, self-mutilation as a release and punishment began to escalate toward addiction. I would see how many cuts I could make until I couldn't stand it or how many I could do before stopping. When cutting was no longer enough, I looked for other ways to injure myself to the extent that I burned my flesh with a curling iron. This proved to be too painful and didn't last long.

A few weeks after I'd moved out, I went to visit a friend. She took one look at me and said, "What's going on?"

"What do you mean?" She repeated the question. Her tone warned me she wouldn't let me off easy.

"I finally found my relief," I confessed and pulled up my pant leg to reveal at least a dozen slice marks, a couple as fresh as the day before.

Her eyes were as big as saucers, and she covered her mouth with her hand. There was no question that it was wide open with shock as well.

I instantly regretted my impromptu show-and-tell scene.

Perhaps she saw that, too, because she quickly recovered. "Hey, if you ever need to talk or if you need anything, just let me know. I'm always here for you."

From that day on, for the sake of control, I kept what I did hidden, never wearing skirts or shorts. What drew more attention was the change in my appearance. I went in for the whole "goth" look with loose, dark clothing and intense black makeup. I assumed a dark, withdrawn iden-

not by chance

tity and guarded my privacy. I seemed to be making friends with my lifelong enemy, isolation.

One day, my parents dropped by unexpectedly. Unaware it was them, I grabbed a pair of shorts and a t-shirt to throw on before answering the door. I wore a silver pentagram, a common satanic symbol, on a chain around my neck.

"My God, Jill," Mom gasped when she saw me. She looked at my legs. "What's happened to you? Do you want to move back home?"

There was neither the need nor the desire, of course, on my part. They were deeply concerned and over the next few weeks, launched an all-out campaign to bring me home.

***

It was time to get out of Wheatland. Besides the conflict with my parents, every place I turned in town reminded me of things that Hannah and I had done together. Living alone reminded me of plans we'd made that had not panned out. Weighing my options, I went online and found a cooking school in Scottsdale, Arizona. To my pleasant surprise, I was accepted within days, and I wasted no time in getting ready to go.

In the back of my mind, I knew I was out of control. Some friends urged me to get help. With counseling and antidepressants, the urges to hurt myself and even to take my own life were far less frequent. By January, we thought

home

I was good to go, to start fresh at Scottsdale Culinary Institute.

The first three or four months were great, and I thought maybe I had turned a corner. Eventually, the initial excitement wore off, and when it did, feelings of isolation and hopelessness washed over me like a tidal wave. All the problems I'd left in Wyoming came back to haunt me. There was an endless stream of roommates as we were shuffled over and over for various reasons. Although I'd always wanted friends, I was generally quiet and reserved. I wasn't into the partying, drinking and drugs that surrounded me. Having conformed to the expectations of others all my life, I was in a new place where there were no expectations whatsoever, and I was lost.

I turned to two things that had given me the most comfort, witchcraft and cutting. By the time I had a vacation in July, I called my counselor and said, "You have to put me in lockdown when I come home. I'm suicidal, I'm cutting myself more, and I'm freaking everyone out to no end. I mean, I need to get this under control."

"Okay, get down here."

Choosing to spend my vacation in Casper in lockdown devastated my parents and friends. Only I was aware that had I not made this choice, I would not have survived much longer. There, I felt safe and secure. I had no worries. Even the expenses were covered because it was voluntary. Once again, with the help of antidepressants and counseling, I thought I was prepared for anything as I returned to school.

not by chance

As before, the first months comforted me with routine and focus. Then things turned for the better.

***

1,400 miles of wide-open beauty stretched before me, and my heart would dance and sing the whole way. The joy and fresh hope of unconditional love grew as I anticipated finally being face to face with Jake. The familiar red, gold and orange of the Southwest scenery invited me to relive galloping adventures with Penny. Always, they left me breathless and exhilarated. That's how I felt now. This time, I sped across Arizona and Texas in a '94 Ford Mustang, from Scottsdale to El Paso, with the windows down and the wind blowing through my newly blackened goth haircut. Freedom and promise shortened the long hours. Memories of Penny and visions of uniting with my perfect soul mate kept me company. With each mile, my escape from loneliness seemed more certain.

I'd met Jake online several months earlier. For me, it was like meeting someone at the bar or in a grocery store. Anticipation made my heart race each time I thought of hearing from him or even seeing him online. Jake was gothic with long, dark hair, tattoos and several piercings — just the sort of guy I'd have been interested in at home. Virtual dating was, to me, the real deal. We had the Web camera and the microphone as well as the telephone and, in a short time, we were head over heels in love.

My car needed work, and I had to write some bad

home

checks to come up with gas money, but it was worth it to be with this wonderful man and bring him back to Arizona.

He wore tight dark jeans and a white tank t-shirt that revealed muscled arms bearing more tattoos than I'd seen in my life. His hair was loose on his tan shoulders, and he was smoking. Hearing the car in the drive, he turned. I was out of the car almost before putting it in park. A huge grin spread across his face. The studs in his ears, nose, eyebrow and lower lip all sparkled but not as much as his brown eyes. In one motion, he was tossing his cigarette to the ground and wrapping me up in his arms.

A week after we came back from El Paso to Scottsdale, Jake proposed. The romance hadn't stopped since I'd picked him up in Texas. This ultimate bad boy had swept me off my feet.

"Thank you, God, for giving me the man of my dreams," I prayed. I'd never been as happy as I was at that moment.

A moment was really all that it would ever be. Jake had serious drug problems, ranging from pot to meth. Because I loved him and wasn't into drugs, had never been into drugs, I was convinced I could help him.

He made it clear, "This is what I am. This is part of me, and it's never gonna leave."

I told him that if he wanted to leave it, he would choose to leave it. Six rocky months later, he left me instead. First, he moved out of my place and in across the street with his drug dealer. We saw each other a couple of

not by chance

times a week. I had no idea where I stood in the relationship. The nagging fear of losing someone I loved returned. I punished myself repeatedly with cutting. Then Jake planned a two-week vacation to visit family in Seattle. He packed up all his stuff and half of mine and took off. A couple of days later, I checked in at his job. His boss told me Jake had quit and said he was not coming back.

I crashed hard. Blinded in love, I'd been humiliated and abandoned. Too broken to deal with school, I called my parents. They came, picked me up, and I moved in with them. That, in itself, signaled the depths of my despair. I'd lost the desire to live and with it the emotional energy to fight. My mom and dad could not understand what had happened to me. I did work hard to earn enough to move out on my own again. Conflict danced like a flame held to a fuse, waiting to ignite.

Sheri was happy to have me back at *Terragrano*. Life returned to normal, with the exception that I was deeper than ever in depression. While I cut myself over and over, I began to think about suicide as the only way to rid myself of the torment. There were 257 scars on my body from cutting. Only seven of them were on my left arm. The rest were from my waist down. I kept my self-inflicted wounds covered, but the darkness was written all over my face. I was emptiness and death in slow motion.

Wicca became more than just a pastime now. I had become a faithful follower. I found a local mentor. I bought a Ouija board, tarot cards and a crystal ball and learned how to use them. I couldn't admit it was really not

home

giving me what I wanted. I wanted to be free. I wanted to know who I was. There was nothing to take its place in my life, though. At least it gave me an illusion of identity and control.

At my lowest point, I made a pact with Satan to give him complete control of my life if he would kill my parents. In that moment, I realized that I had crossed a line. Up to that time, I believed that I was just dabbling.

"Satan, Lucifer, do what you will with me," I said aloud, so that God would hear how angry I was.

Not too long after that, Sheri pulled me aside at work. We'd always gotten along really well. Lately, we couldn't even work the same shift without being at each other's throats.

"What's happened to you, Jill?"

"I don't know what you're talking about. I'm fine." I'd said it so many times, I was starting to believe it.

"You've changed," she went on. "Something is wrong. You are following something that is evil and something that is dark, and you are headed only for destruction."

She was right.

***

It was the worst week of my life. An inner battle had begun the minute the Campbells told me they were to have a Sunday night gathering for their church people at the house. I'd gone to their cute little church one time when I first returned to Scottsdale and then vowed to have

not by chance

nothing to do with it. Living with Ben, Sara and their children had been my last resort. I'd done everything to try and make other arrangements. When my mother connected with the Campbells through a lady she worked for, my thoughts had been, *No way, I'll die before I'll live with a church family.*

But six tenuous weeks had passed since I'd moved in with them. Their door had opened along with an opportunity to go back to school and move forward with my life, rather than stay home. I reached an agreement with myself to make it work just long enough to get on my feet again.

In that week before the church gathering, I received news that pushed that day further out and me deeper in depression and bitterness.

"I'm sorry." The registrar shook her head and looked over her sliver-shaped reading glasses at me. "You just don't have the academic credit to stay in the program."

"What am I supposed to do?" I asked, knowing she wasn't going to give me an answer. I was stunned. I couldn't bear that my last option was being taken away.

***

"Jill, are you ready to do this tonight?" Pastor Tom looked me straight in the eye. I wanted to hate him. I wanted to cast a spell on him. I wanted to hide.

"I don't know what you mean," I lied.

"I know and you know that you are struggling," he said gently. "You want to have peace. You want to have

home

freedom. Why not just receive it from God?"

Receive? From God? What would God want to give me?

Before I knew it, I was arguing with God while the meeting went on. I was aware of two choices. The way I was living was in darkness, in rebellion, in struggle, in loneliness and isolation. I'd always seen this as God's doing. He had made my life horrible by taking away everything and everyone I loved — the ranch, Penny, Hannah, my home, my dreams, my fiancé, now my school and career. A new thought was entering in my mind: *Could I have missed something?*

Stubbornness prevailed.

"I'm fine," I kept saying afterwards. I wanted to scream, "I'd be just fine if all of you would just leave me alone!"

"I need to drive my wife home," Pastor Tom made one last effort, "but I will come back if you like."

That would be kind of stupid, I thought, *Why would he need to do that?*

I said, "I'm fine."

He waved goodnight to Sara who had stepped out from the kitchen. Ben had carried something to someone's car and was heading in as the pastor was leaving. I watched them shake hands.

Suddenly, I was overcome with fear as never before. I saw Jake leaving. I saw Hannah leaving. I heard the gate close behind our truck. It was not God who had taken those things away. He'd been right there with me, instead,

not by chance

ready to fill the emptiness. He offered light and hope and life. The choice was incredibly clear: light or darkness, fulfillment or emptiness, life or death. It was *my* choice. I *was* in control. Struggling against God seemed silly and fruitless all of a sudden. He offered to give me something real, real friendship, real power, real control.

Pastor was stepping out the door. "Wait," I nearly shouted. "Will you come back?"

He smiled and laid his hand on my shoulder. "I'll be back in about 20 minutes."

He was. By the time he got back, I was like a blind person whose eyes had been opened. I'd been wandering around in darkness, thinking that it brought comfort and peace. It was now so obvious that the direction I was headed in was destruction, misery and death. I saw it as I did in the park four years earlier. But this time, I felt it, and I was terrified that there may not be another chance of escape.

"The thief comes to steal, kill and destroy; but I have come that you might have life and that life to the full." I had seen God as a taker. The very things that I was grasping to hold, he'd been trying to give me in himself.

When Pastor Tom returned and asked again, "Jill, are you ready to do this tonight?" I calmly agreed.

"Yes, yes, yes," I kept saying, as he asked me if I wanted peace, joy, love, fulfillment. "Yes, I confess my sins; I renounce Satan and witchcraft."

"Yes." I chose light.

"Yes." I chose life.

home

"Yes." I chose peace.

I responded calmly and honestly. "Yes, I am ready to come back to God and ready to turn away from Lucifer himself."

I knelt in the living room to surrender to God and to renounce the devil. "Lord Jesus," I prayed, "I repent of my sin, and I ask your forgiveness. Wash me clean and make me a new person in your likeness."

As I confessed, I felt a rush of relief and then peace like I'd never felt before. Barely aware of anyone in the room, in a moment, I sensed that Ben and Sara were standing with the pastor, praying over me. They prayed for my release from the evil that was holding me. At the same time, I envisioned releasing it.

Then it dawned on me. I was doing something I hadn't done in what seemed like a thousand years. I was crying. Tears were spilling down my face in a wave of release. It felt so good. I closed my eyes and embraced the peace and light. I cried for repentance, and then I cried for joy.

***

Each day, I'm sensing how much God adores me, that to lose me would break his heart. When I encounter rejection or loss, I realize he stands with me and cries for those who walk away from him. When I am heartbroken, I can run to him and cry in his arms. I appealed to be readmitted to the culinary school and was turned down. But I instantly felt the comfort that God was in control and had

not by chance

other plans, better plans for me. I stayed with the Campbells and received their love and the love of an extended church family.

The scars from cutting have almost healed, and I've not felt the need to punish myself since that night I cried to the Lord. He shed his own blood for me. His scars remain as a reminder of this.

I've broken free of the bondage of Wicca. What I thought brought me control, imprisoned me instead. I don't want to hide in darkness anymore. I want to continue to walk in light and peace. Even though darkness and despair may surround me, I choose to trust him to keep me safe. I may not know what is happening next or have the ability to manipulate it to satisfy myself, but I know that my huge and magnificent God is in control, and he has my best interests at heart.

I've left the isolation to receive a far better companion in Jesus Christ. We are inseparable because he now lives within me. Daily, I am able to walk and talk with him and share my joy and sorrow.

"Jill, what's happened to you? You've changed," my friends say now with smiles and open hearts.

I don't have to lie when I answer, "God has changed me. I'm happier than I've ever been."

This wild spirit has found her best friend and a place of belonging. From here, I am learning to quickly respond to the gentle tug of the Lord's rein on my heart. I don't mind the fences, the stalls or the barn. I'm home, and I belong.

conclusion

I trust at least a flicker of hope has been ignited within you, for either yourself or for someone you know who has faced similar, painful experiences. These stories are representative of many in our Two Rivers family who have experienced genuine life change through a personal encounter with their creator, God.

If you have honest questions or doubts if such life-changing experiences are possible, each of us warmly extends an invitation to you to come and check out our church family. Freely ask questions, examine our reality factor, and if you choose, journey with us at whatever pace you are comfortable with. We just want you to know God is still completing the process of authentic life change in us, so we still make mistakes in our journey, like everyone will. Therefore, we acknowledge our continued need for each other's forgiveness and support.

If you are unable to be with us, yet you intuitively sense you would really like to experience such a life change, here are some fundamental essentials to consider. If you choose, at the end, say the suggested prayer. If your prayer genuinely comes from your innermost being, you can expect to experience the beginning stages of authentic life change, similar to those you have read about.

Acknowledge you have broken God's laws, and unless he forgives you, you will be forever separated from him. Romans 6:23: "The reward for sin is death, but the gift that God freely gives is everlasting life found in Christ Jesus

not by chance

our Lord."

Believe in your heart God passionately loves you and wants to give you a new heart. Ezekiel 11:19: "I will give them singleness of heart and put a new spirit within them. I will take away their stony, stubborn heart and give them a tender, responsive heart." NLT

Believe in your heart that, "If you confess with your mouth that Jesus is Lord and believe in your heart that God raised him from the dead, you will be saved." Romans 10:9 NLT

Believe in your heart that because Jesus paid for you breaking God's law, and because you asked him to forgive you, he has filled your new heart with his life in such a way that he transforms you from the inside out. 2 Corinthians 5:17: "When someone becomes a Christian, he becomes a brand new person inside. He is not the same anymore. A new life has begun!" TLB

Pray this suggested prayer as if it was yours: "Lord Jesus, I know I am separated from you, but I want to change that. I am sorry for the choices I've made that have broken your laws. I believe your death paid for my sins, and you are now alive to change me from the inside out. Would you please do that now? Thank you for hearing and changing me. Now, please help me know when you are talking to me, so I can cooperate with your efforts to change me. Amen."

We would love for you to join us!
We meet Sunday mornings at 10 a.m. at
645 N. Gilbert Road, Suite 180,
Gilbert, Arizona 85234.

Please call us at 480.892.2435 for directions, or contact us at www.2riverschurch.org.

For more information on reaching your city with stories from your church, please contact Good Catch Publishing at www.goodcatchpublishing.com

Good Catch Publishing